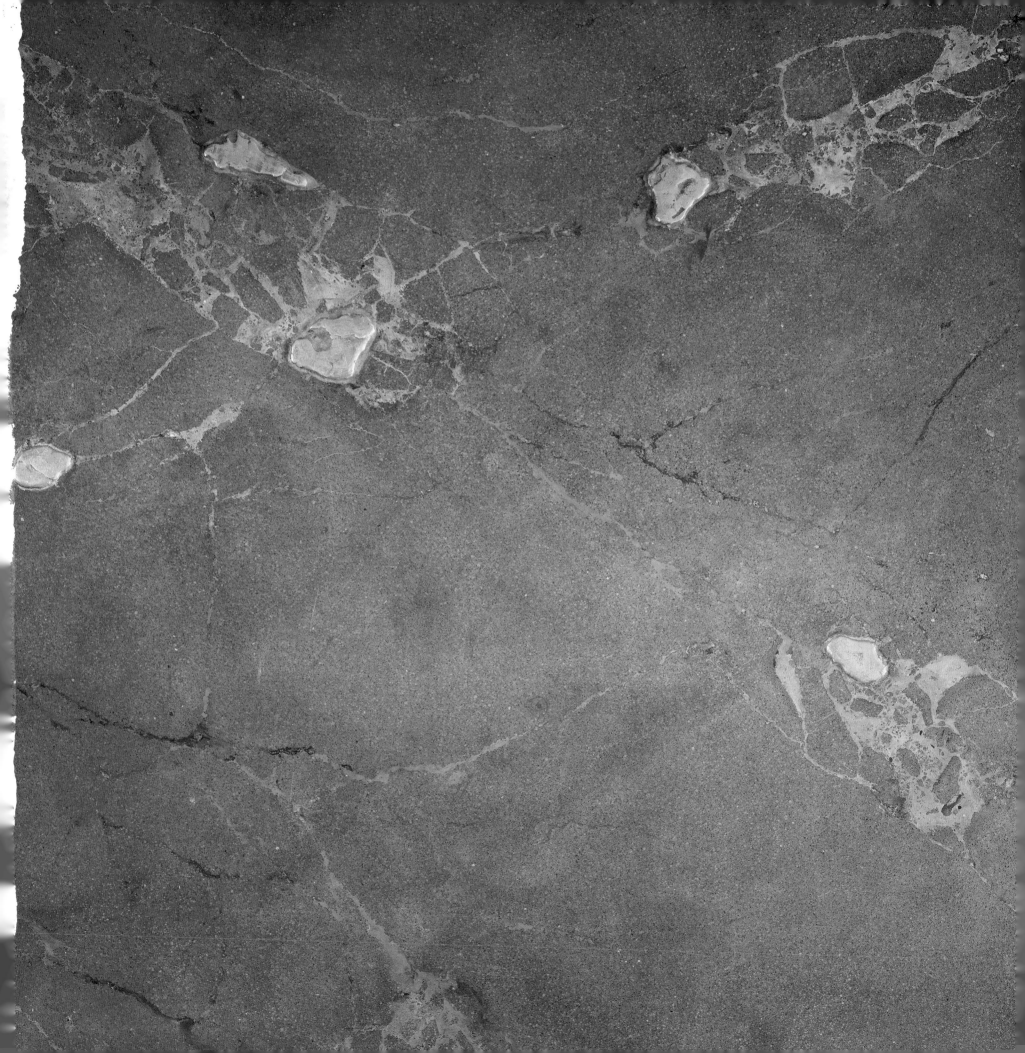

KITCHEN

to Blair

Mick DéGiulio

Dec 17 2010

CENTRIC

Mick De Giulio

with Karen Klages Grace

**Introduction by
Christopher G. Kennedy**

Balcony Press

CONTENTS

Photograph 5 by Julian Wass for House Beautiful magazine, 2009; photograph 11 used with permission from Beautiful Kitchens magazine

PREFACE

I do not remember exactly when Mick De Giulio and I first met.

It was probably in Milan at a design show and not in Chicago where both he and I are based. But it definitely followed years of superlatives. One of my former colleagues at the *Chicago Tribune*, a more senior reporter of design and the decorative arts, would precede his name with lauds of "extraordinary" and "exquisite" whenever she did a story on kitchens. The rest of us knew him by default—and by the lush photographs of his work.

Mick De Giulio creates extraordinary kitchens, dream kitchens. He is known internationally for his kitchens and likewise for a growing collection of products under his own label and for other companies including SieMatic of Germany and Kallista, a Kohler company, of Kohler, Wisconsin. His Hudson Valley line of cabinetry for SieMatic was chosen for a 2002 renovation of the Blair House in Washington, D.C. His polished stainless steel range hoods (for the de Giulio Collection) look like pieces of modern sculpture, his carved stone sinks like they were lifted from Italian villas.

Mick brings fantasy and couture to the world of kitchens, but I believe he has done more than that. He has shown the rest of us that kitchens can be more than a standard assembly of countertops, cabinets, and appliances. Kitchens can be artful compositions and expressions of ourselves. And they can be rooms not just where we chop, dice, roast, and sauté, but rooms we *live* in, places at once inspired and inspiring.

In this book, Mick takes readers on a guided tour through eighteen of his favorite kitchen projects from around the United States. They are in city apartments and lofts, suburban houses, manor houses, seaside homes, design showrooms, a mountain retreat, and one restored horse barn. He tells the inside story—the making—of each of these kitchens, which roll one after the other like short films. The Decoded chapter provides specific information on the materials and products used in each of them. The Tenets chapter reveals Mick's basic beliefs.

To me, the real glory of this book is its power to inspire. Everyone with a dream kitchen in mind—those who can afford big-ticket kitchens and those of modest means—can look to this book for ideas on mixing different woods, stones, metals, colors, and looks in the same kitchen. Perennial questions about whether stainless steel, white kitchens, and granite are "out" are answered visually with a decided "no" and a call for getting creative.

Grab something interesting to drink, find a comfortable chair, and do not forget the sticky notes to flag pages. Your dream kitchen is about to begin.

Karen Klages Grace

INTRODUCTION

The Heart of the Home and the Community

Christopher G. Kennedy

A half-century ago the Midwest was the center of America's isolationist movement, and Chicago was the very heart of Fortress America. But a great conversion, accelerated by architects, artists, and designers, occurred and changed every aspect of life. Their work not only changed Chicago's self-image, but opened up a creative exchange between America's Midwest and the rest of the world.

I don't think it was merely accidental or coincidental that one of the great architects of the international school of architecture, Ludwig Mies van der Rohe, along with the many talented Chicago architects who embraced his ideas, were transforming Chicago's architecture while the city simultaneously transformed itself from a backward-looking, fearful community into a strong, capable city known for its modern influence on a changing world. Architecture and design expanded Chicago's presence in the international community and its pioneering spirit opened the minds of Chicago residents. As the design communities embraced Chicago's newfound recognition and confidence, the business community followed suit, gaining international presence and success for our city.

Today, Chicago sends innovations of the American Heartland to port cities from Rotterdam to Osaka. We dominate world markets from London to Tokyo with the products of our financial exchanges, while Chicago-based companies like Exelon, Baxter, and Motorola lead the world in energy, health care, and technology.

Still today, great design has the potential to transform our community ensuring that we continue not only to embrace new ideas but to generate them, to welcome fresh concepts and fear no change.

Just as great architects transformed Chicago life in the mid-twentieth century, Mick De Giulio helped lead a design revolution of another kind. Fostering creativity and beauty amid structure, he helped form the philosophy that homes—particularly kitchens—are not only where family is defined, but also the place where we determine the future of our larger community.

Through his work, Mick has demonstrated that families are not simply buying kitchen cabinets, but ensuring a critical environment for good and investing in their future. He has helped to reveal the important truth that homes serve a greater purpose. Central to building togetherness and community, homes help us solidify our faith in interaction and carry its value out into the world.

The significance of the home as a communal gathering place has helped encourage the creation of public gathering places for the Chicago community. Chicago is committed to building community spaces. In recent years Chicago built the Harris Theater and renovated and restored its Civic Opera House. Chicago constructed Millennium Park with a focus on bringing together art, design, and green space. Chicago dedicated resources to attract the Joffrey Ballet to the city and recently welcomed the opening of the Modern Wing at the Art Institute of Chicago.

All of these places reflect and strengthen community. They are places for people of all backgrounds to come together to share new ideas and discuss current issues in art, music, theater, nature, and civic life.

This larger commitment to communal spaces stems from commitments that began with smaller groups throughout the Chicago area—in the homes of individuals who were leaders in their families and communities.

Through the work of Mick De Giulio, we have seen the modern kitchen evolve from a back-of-the-house place of efficiency into a welcoming environment that is central to decision making, entertaining, and sharing.

We have seen great design in the home transform the way families, schools, parishes, neighborhoods, and communities interact—how they inspire and improve the lives of people all over the world.

Homes have been the foundation of families for generations. While families may try to draw traffic to other rooms, the kitchen always seems to be the most comfortable central gathering place in any home. Families gather for holidays, spending most of the time in the kitchen, catching up with one another as they cook and bake their traditional fare and reaffirm their familial bond. De Giulio kitchens have certainly played a significant role over the years in shaping the style and memories of family traditions.

Homes have also become a welcoming venue for members of churches and temples and grade school parent organizations. The kitchen fosters productivity and exchange. Deepest thoughts are shared, improvements are debated, and changes are implemented at the kitchen tables of the participants in these important support systems.

The ability of a home to build a familial bond stretches to the school community as well. Homes have become central to high school sports' team-building activities off the field, such as team dinners hosted by parents. Sharing a meal at a kitchen table reminds everyone a team is a kind of family, too, and allows these young adults to build camaraderie and confidence and to strengthen their spirit.

We have seen great design of the home act as a catalyst for change in our larger community as well.

Fundraisers for our city's major improvements such as the Civic Opera or the Jay Pritzker Pavilion at Millennium Park are often staged in the homes of civic leaders.

The home has also become a place to define our future at a national level. When Barack Obama began his grassroots Senate campaign, his early supporters hosted him in their homes. Many special events, fundraisers, dinners, and cocktail parties took place in de Giulio kitchens, paving the way for interactive discussion and a campaign based on this dedication to community—building and change accomplished through shared effort.

Mick De Giulio understands the important role of the physical structure of the home in our society. With great design, a dedication to tranquility and beauty, and a commitment to the function of community-building, de Giulio kitchens have a role in shaping who we are and what we value, providing us with a context not only for interaction and kinship but with something soulful—the great potential that always accompanies coming together in familial ways, celebrating the heart of the home as the essential center of a strong society.

Christopher G. Kennedy is president of Merchandise Mart Properties Inc. (MMPI), a division of Vornado Realty Trust. MMPI owns and/or manages sixteen properties nationwide, including The Merchandise Mart in Chicago and the Architects & Designers building in New York, and produces more than three hundred events, trade and consumer shows, and conferences each year.

KITCHEN SOUP

Rachel Kohler

I did not expect my new kitchen to be the wonderful cure-all that it has become.

The story begins with a space problem. We were living in a typical city house—a vertical stack of space. Things were fine when Mara was born. They got a bit more crowded when Lena came along. By this time, we noticed many of our friends with two kids moving to the suburbs. With two Chicago-based careers and a love of the city, we decided to stay put. But then Leo came along. After breathing deeply and reaffirming our commitment to city life, we moved the girls into the same room and integrated Leo. As the girls grew, it became apparent that sharing a small room and a really small closet wasn't going to work. So we sacrificed the last semblance of graciousness and converted the guestroom into a grown-up girl abode for Mara. Needless to say, we did not know many other families of five living in Lincoln Park.

When the grandparents started staying at hotels during their visits to Chicago, and it was more exhausting to remove the large plastic toys from the living room than to entertain guests, we knew we had to move. Easier said than done.

After over two years of searching for the right combination of design, location, and availability, we finally found what we were looking for. OK, I have to admit, the property does cover four city lots. Maybe we, or at least I, were a bit more traumatized by our close quarters than I cared to admit. The house, built by a couple of art lovers to showcase their significant collection, had space, space, and more space. We embraced the notion of turning it into a family home even though it meant putting an addition onto the already large residence. Also, while the house was in generally fabulous condition, the kitchen was not. In fact, I was quite surprised that two people and a dog could put so much wear and tear on a room. I didn't dwell on this at the time but instead felt lucky that the kitchen was one of the very few renovations we would have to do to the existing structure. And, frankly, I could steel myself against anything—even building and rehabbing in the city—just to have my space.

The architecture of the house bears no embellishment. Less prevails. The only thing in abundance from an architectural standpoint is walls—long, tall walls designed for hanging giant pieces of art. Light darts across those walls through carefully placed windows. Large, tall-ceilinged rooms flow from one to the next. All around there is this profound sense of *space*. Not just elbowroom, the space I'm talking about is a larger kind of heady room. The modern architecture made the house a blank canvas, and it made me feel like I could breathe and think and be at peace with my things instead of being constantly at war with them.

In our project, we were willing to decouple the interior design of the rest of the house from the kitchen. We wanted a kitchen expert. Growing up in the Kohler plumbing family made me appreciate the power of a core competency. We sought a person who understood the specifics of a kitchen space but also how to bring beauty to it. Working in the home furnishings industry means constantly being exposed to beautiful rooms and beautiful things. Our new home finally offered an opportunity to fully explore our own sense of this. We were serious about ensuring we had all the benefits our previous kitchen deprived us of. Specifically, we had no room for extra sets of dishes or glassware. No room for small appliances. No room to enjoy a meal with the whole family unless enduring a squeeze at the kitchen table. Mick De Giulio was a person who clearly understood how to accomplish all the functions without sacrificing any form.

We skip forward two years, and it is finally time to move. Unfortunately, my big relief felt like something different to our children. What had become an unbearable squeeze for my husband and me was to our children normal and safe. To them the closeness was comfort and security.

After a bit of bitter complaining, they resorted to wandering aimlessly. Maybe those big walls made them feel especially small. Maybe it was the newness of it all. Whatever it was, they could not find their comfort zone. But interestingly enough, they did find the kitchen. There was something about the kitchen in our new home that called to them and comforted them like a bowl of chicken soup, and it still does. I have no doubt that my presence in the kitchen, which is where I go when I get home, is a big part of that calling. Children want to be near their mother, but it seems to go further than that. The kitchen provided the intimacy they missed.

This kitchen has become the center of our family life. Thankfully, the kids have gotten comfortable in the rest of the house, but the kitchen is where they gravitate. They do their homework at the kitchen table, even though there is a nice little study room off the kitchen proper. We read in the kitchen, even though there are plenty of more comfortable reading places in the house. We carve pumpkins at the kitchen table. We make piñatas and build Legos in the kitchen. Because of the "no TV on a school night" rule, we are apt to be in the kitchen at night, quizzing for a test or playing games. My son makes sport out of opening and closing the automatic shade on the big skylight over the island. He loves pressing that button on the control and imagining that he can touch the sky. And somehow, beyond my wildest imagination, cooking with my children on weekends has become *my* hobby, time with my family, in our kitchen.

I ask myself: "How did *this* happen?" And then I realize that this kitchen has happened to other people, too. When we entertain, our guests inevitably end up in the kitchen, at the island. My husband and I, even without our kids or guests, have become kitchen-bent as well. Mark has a home office but he often likes to work at the kitchen table. On Sunday nights, after the kids are in bed, I go to the kitchen to cozy up with a cup of tea to read the week's mail.

Perhaps that is the secret power of our kitchen. Its beauty is multidimensional. The room has natural light and proportions that make a person feel both comfortable and important in the space. In some ways, renovation of a room is a more difficult assignment for a designer than a complete teardown. We did not ask Mick to start over; we asked him to enhance the qualities of our good kitchen. Mick, of course, recognized this and didn't feel he needed to gut the space but rather to just tweak it to achieve our objectives. This egoless approach is signature Mick.

We agreed the cabinets needed to be replaced but should remain a light color. We selected oak. It made the modern look in the kitchen even more tactile and friendly. Mick suggested a larger island with pullout drawers for kid-friendly access. Now the kids can participate in kitchen duties. Everybody saddles up to that island, which is now a more substantial element in the kitchen as well as a more forgiving one. The former island had a monolithic marble topping. The marble had no seams and incredible veining. It was stunning, and I hated to lose it, but I did not want to be fretting over stained marble. Mick came up with a great solution: granite, which is harder and more stain-resistant than marble. We kept the original look by selecting a monolithic piece of granite with no seams and gorgeous graining and then mitered the edges of it to make it appear thicker.

Mick chose stainless steel for the counters and appliances. He also suggested running a stainless steel shelf across the entire back wall. The stainless steel makes the kitchen feel less precious, more accessible, and friendlier.

The existing skylight is wonderful during the day, but at night it is a big black hole. Mick worked with our architects to add lights inside the skylight and additional recessed lights throughout the kitchen and pantry. The new scheme makes the room feel alive at any time of the day.

Perhaps my favorite part of the kitchen is the built-in wall cabinets. Mick came up with a design plan that gives me enough space to house my linens, my flatware, three sets of dinnerware (each has service for twenty), and multiple sets of stemware. That space is an incredible gift. Everything I need is at my fingertips. I do not have to go downstairs or upstairs or in a remote closet to find something. I can be more creative with my table settings and entertaining, without searching for what I would like to use. He also didn't flinch at accommodating a beloved piece of artwork and our array of electronic gadgets but figured out creative ways of making it all fit in seamlessly.

At the end of the day, our kitchen is a gift to our family…it gives us each something—intimacy, sanity, and of course, beauty. It is not just about the beauty *of* the space but how we live more beautifully *in* the space and *because of* the space.

Rachel Kohler is group president— interiors (which includes Baker Knapp & Tubbs, McGuire, Mark David, Ann Sacks, and Kallista brands) of Kohler Company. She also is a member of the Kohler Company Board of Directors.

THE KITCHEN ERA

James Bakke

People who follow design might not devote much time to the late twentieth century. But from my vantage point, the era that gave us laissez-faire economics, political correctness, prosperity, new wave music, and new media also gave Americans a new take on the kitchen. The kitchen emerged in glory across this country as a room of high performance, high design, and even artfulness—and nothing about this room has been the same since. In short, Americans have come to design their home life around a room that's no longer about drudgery and all about dreams.

I comment from the perspective of a third-generation family businessman. My family has been in the refrigeration business since the 1940s and in cooking since 2000. We make upscale refrigerators and freezers, cooktops, ovens, and ranges, which gives me a front-row seat on the changing kitchen tide over the last fifty-plus years. I happen to believe that innovations in major appliances have driven the most profound changes in the kitchen over the last century—that and a couple of key groups of people who had the passion to take those advances and essentially change the American home. But I will get to that later.

Certainly, the early decades of the twentieth century were full of radical culinary invention. Electric refrigerators (replacing the old iceboxes), gas stoves, electric stoves—they all drastically changed the way the kitchen functioned and how it looked. The kitchen was a spiffier place, all right, but it was still the kitchen, a workhorse room.

The 1940s saw its share of invention too, including the freestanding, chest-style home freezer, an appliance pioneered by my grandfather, Westye Bakke, who launched the Sub-Zero Freezer Company in 1945 with that as his signature piece. Advances in upright freezer design, styling, and colors followed, as did an overall, postwar taste for design and glamour. The 1950s brought slick-looking ovens and ranges, better dishwashers, and a fledgling concept that would come to change everything: built-in refrigeration. It allowed refrigeration, which was considered the ugly duckling of major appliances, to slide into cabinetry and virtually disappear. And hence, the prospect of a streamlined kitchen was born. But again, the kitchen was still the kitchen, still a room of utility.

Things started to change in the 1960s when the Hollywood crowd discovered the joys and status of the ever-advancing, state-of-the-art kitchen, and the media was hot to show and tell the story. But it was not until the late 1970s and more like the 1980s and '90s that change really took hold, that a more mainstream America got a taste for and taste of the glory kitchen, which was as much about style and lifestyle as it was about function.

A confluence of events and people made that happen, most notably some forward-thinking builders in a hot, southern California real estate market. They were installing upscale kitchens not just in their model homes and custom homes, but in tract homes. Remodelers on the East Coast also were installing glory kitchens, and so were Floridians. About the same time, a European influence had hit the United States in everything from cars to clothes to kitchens. Sophisticated German and Italian kitchens (made of simple woods and laminates) gave Americans something fresh and new: clean, modern kitchens that looked like fashion.

And then came the expansion of kitchen dealerships across the country, many of which found they could sell the more expensive, more fantastic kitchens. They had professionals on staff, people who could create the magic — the kitchen designers — who, though certainly not in a new profession, seemed to coalesce as a group and come of age at that moment.

In 1994, my company gave those dealers and designers another bit of magic to further transform the kitchen: integrated refrigeration. It took the concept of built-in refrigeration to a new level of frameless, seamless integration. It turned the refrigerator and freezer into compartments and drawers that could be installed anywhere in a kitchen or house for that matter. And to my mind, it gave kitchen designers artistic license to turn the kitchen into something that need not look like a kitchen anymore.

At Sub-Zero, we knew we were on to something. But when designers such as Mick De Giulio started designing and building incredible cabinets (which looked like antiques or were antiques or were clean-lined, modern pieces) to house our integrated products and in the process turned these custom kitchens into fantastic rooms that rivaled any other *living* room in the house in both looks and comfort, I really knew we had something with our integrated line.

And I knew Mick De Giulio (whom I have known for probably twenty years now) and others like him at the top of the design profession had something, too — the vision to reinvent the kitchen as the center of the American home and not just a room of utility. Perhaps Mick had a leg up on things. He was a part of our development team for the integrated line and has been involved in a number of subsequent product development sessions, including our decision to add high-end cooking to our lineup, which we did with the acquisition of the Wolf Gourmet brand in 2000. Mick was influential in helping us design a whole collection of Wolf products. He also has brought our products to life for us in a big way. He has designed kitchens for our showrooms and for our world-class training center in Madison, Wisconsin.

But I think it is more than Mick having an insider perspective. Mick is not just a designer. He is a good dreamer, and he is an artist. And he gets it. He gets that the kitchen has come out of the back room. It is a room to be lived in and loved — a place to gather and break bread with style and grace.

James Bakke is president and chief executive officer of Sub-Zero/Wolf, based in Madison, Wisconsin.

MY CENTRICITY

There is a quote from Pablo Picasso that I really like: "Everything you can imagine is real." I relate to that, because I have spent my entire career imagining the unreal. I imagine kitchens that sing. Some of my best voices (my best come-true kitchens) are on the next 200-plus pages.

I believe a great kitchen has a magic to it that transforms the physical room into a *feeling*. The great kitchen has a spirit, an aura, an intangible that is real. People are drawn to that kitchen, and they may not know why. The kitchen sings.

It is my job (and has been for more than three decades now) to write the music. I may call myself a kitchen designer, but what I really do is orchestrate and conduct the dreaming process. I listen to my clients, absorb, and then jump aboard their excitement, sometimes leading, sometimes following, but always steering that energy into both tangible and intangible—a kitchen that feeds the soul.

Why design, why kitchens, and why kitchens that sing?

Circumstances of my youth put me on the path to becoming a woodworker and then a designer. But early on, I got turned on by the power of the kitchen. I began to see the kitchen as being central to a person's and a family's well-being.

This is where the "centric" idea comes into play. I am kitchen centric, for sure. My entire professional life has been centered on kitchens. But I also believe very strongly that American homes and home life have been becoming kitchen centric too. As the twenty-first century unfolds, I believe we are going to see the kitchen continue to evolve into the emotional center of the home, if not the spatial one.

In some ways, we have come full circle as humans. There is precedence for kitchen centricity. In the Middle Ages, European longhouses, for instance, had one big room (and perhaps another small room for sleeping) with a fireplace in the center for cooking, warming, and lighting. In Colonial America, the kitchen was not a separate room. It existed in the corner of the cabin. And much more recently, in the late twentieth century, homebuilders were touting something they called the open kitchen, where the wall between the kitchen and family room came down. The open

Mick De Giulio

kitchen acknowledged that people were spending more time in the kitchen, so why not incorporate it into the family space? The problem was with the execution, as the family room became a cavernous place and the kitchen got tucked away, sometimes with little or no natural light, in the back of this hall-like space. The kitchen was an addendum.

My mission has been to create kitchens that are the palpable heart of home life. And in some cases (where client and budget are willing) the kitchen turns into the physical hub of the house as well, with space allotted not just for gathering as a family for meals or doing homework at the kitchen table, but for entertaining friends, watching TV, kicking back and reading a book, and even (my personal favorite) taking a nap—because the kitchen *is* the living room.

My wife and I live that way now, but we evolved our kitchen life, just like everyone else. Our kitchen always was a beautiful space and our family's gathering place. When our children were young, we ate in the kitchen, played games, did crafts.

With all four of our kids (nearly) gone from the house, my wife and I looked long and hard at how we live now. We realized we spend most of our waking time in the kitchen and decided to explore new depths of our kitchen centricity.

Granted, we had a good framework in place. Nearly fifteen years ago we added (to our vintage French Normandy just outside of Chicago) the space that is now our kitchen. It includes a sitting/living area, which brought a fireplace, TV, and two comfortable upholstered chairs to our kitchen proper.

Recently, we took that "living" aspect of our kitchen a few steps further. We removed our sixty-inch round kitchen table; it made us feel like too much of our family was missing. (The table went into an adjoining and particularly spacious butler's pantry.) And into our kitchen/living space went two more upholstered chairs and a family heirloom loveseat paired with a much smaller table (we call it a low breakfast table) that I designed and had our shop build using antique French andirons for the base and a top made out of Italian *cottopesto*. This is where my wife and I eat, usually tapas-style. This also is where we entertain close friends. This is where I do my reading and some of my design work and writing. And this is where I like to take a nap, with the fire roaring, on a cold, snowy Chicago day. The kitchen has become our living room.

I have clients who share the desire to grow their kitchen-centered way of life, as well. One of them is building a house in Florida around the kitchen. Everything in the floor plan flows outward from the kitchen. Another client with a much smaller space in a city high-rise turned their 225-square-foot kitchen into the centerpiece of their apartment. They do most of their entertaining around the kitchen island. And another client, a married couple here in suburban Chicago, put their 9,000-square-foot French Provincial house on the market, because they want to build a new house that is more *completely* livable. They are prepared to forgo the salons and formal rooms and get themselves a home where the living area is all one room centered around the kitchen—because that is *how they live*.

OPPOSITE
In addition to creating kitchens, Mick De Giulio designs a growing number of products for both the de Giulio Collection and other companies. Shown here is his BeauxArts collection for SieMatic of Germany. The collection is marked by its clean, simple lines — and its refusal to declare itself either modern or traditional.

Photograph courtesy of SieMatic

THIS PAGE
Over the years, De Giulio and his wife, Andrea, have evolved their kitchen-centered way of living. Nearly fifteen years ago, they added a new kitchen-with-sitting area onto their house in a northern suburb of Chicago. More recently, they turned that sitting area into a comfy spot for a couple of empty nesters. They removed their large family dining table and replaced it with a low breakfast table (of De Giulio's design) and upholstered seating.

Used with permission from *Beautiful Kitchens* magazine

I am not at a loss for words when people ask me what the latest trends are in kitchens, or what I am seeing now. I like to answer in terms of what I am *doing,* and that is always directly related to how my clients live or desire to live. That— lifestyle—is the trend worth heeding.

So, here it is:

I do personality-driven design—design that is more artistic, more creative, full of texture and quirks, which I believe are a good thing.

Most of my kitchens are mixed; they walk the line between traditional and modern without declaring an allegiance to either.

I look at the kitchen holistically—which means not just looking at cabinets, countertops, and backsplashes as the only important elements of the space, but as part of a working whole that connects to the house and also has the feeling or essence of the client.

I am doing more kitchens that incorporate a sitting area, like the one my wife and I now have. For some clients, it turns into a full-fledged living space, although the kitchen is the dominant element. In many cases, that means the kitchen becomes notably bigger.

And for a select but growing group of clients, I am doing kitchens that take in the dining room (admittedly this is not for everyone) to create a larger kitchen where both informal and formal dining occurs. It is for people who brazenly acknowledge that they rarely use the formal dining room and are tired of appropriating a separate space to it.

Clearly, I do luxury kitchens (many in this book are upward of five hundred square feet) for people who can afford their wildest dreams. But a great kitchen is certainly not reserved for the wealthy. Kitchens can sing at all budgets. It is a matter of having a dream and making it work. There are all sorts of wonderful materials and products available today that do not cost a fortune. The harder part is imagining the possibilities, and that is one of the goals of this book—to inspire dreams.

My journey in kitchen design began in the 1950s in Dearborn, Michigan, just outside of Detroit. I grew up immersed in a dichotomous world of craft and industry. My father, John, who remains my inspiration, worked as a tool and die maker at Ford Motor Company. He came to the United States from Italy as a boy, and being from a family of Italian entrepreneurs, he dreamed of owning his own business. In 1969, at the age of forty, he did just that and bought The L&M Cabinet Shop in Royal Oak, Michigan, for five thousand dollars even though he knew little about woodworking. (Tool and die shops were much more costly.) For years, he kept his day job at Ford and moonlighted at the wood shop, where my brothers and I worked after school and on weekends. We built cupolas and octagonal windows for garages—commodity products, nothing to sing about.

But I learned a lot there. I learned about proportion, about joining wood, about different types of wood, and about mixing materials. I learned how to experiment and think creatively and, most important, I learned there is no end to the possibilities when you dream.

Our family expanded the business into kitchens. At the age of nineteen, I designed my first kitchen, under the auspices of my father's shop.

My father left Ford in the mid 1970s to devote full time to his wood shop. A few years later and now a married man, I moved my young family to the Chicago area where I took a job helping run a high-end kitchen design company and shortly after, in 1984, opened de Giulio kitchen design—my own dream and business—on Chicago's North Shore.

At that time, American kitchens were mainly about cabinets, countertops, backsplashes, appliances, and flooring. Pick one, pick the others, and the design process was done. I knew from the start that I wanted to do something different. I wanted to be more creative. I wanted to explore the artistic possibilities and a broader range of materials (natural stones and woods and not just synthetic products).

While traveling to Europe in the early 1980s (especially Germany, Holland, and Italy) to visit factories and attend design shows, I saw the European influence firsthand—sophisticated, contemporary kitchens that energized my creative spirit. I wanted to go back home and do my own take on modern design, mixing materials and vocabularies in new ways with my eye on the artful kitchen.

When I could not find products that I needed, I designed them myself. I started designing my own stone sinks after a trip to Verona, Italy, where I saw a beautiful

De Giulio designed two kitchens
for the Sub-Zero/Wolf training
center in Madison, Wisconsin.
His La Grande kitchen includes
this classical wine room.

400-year-old stone sink. And among my early ideas was a modern take on the appliance garage. It involved taking a double-hung window sash and hardware, mounting cabinet doors to those glassless windows, and installing the whole thing into a backsplash recess. The result was a more beautiful design than the typical, tambour-door appliance garage. I eventually figured out a way to make the sash motorized.

My signature products have grown to become a major part of my work and now include rectangular sinks with sliding cutting boards and accessories atop them; sliding spice walls (usually installed along the range wall) made of marble; refrigerator cabinets that look like Asian armoires or apothecary cabinets; custom range hoods in polished stainless steel; and metal light fixtures and table bases. Most of these products are made at our workshop outside of Chicago and at our metal fabricating facility in Michigan.

I connected with SieMatic of Germany, a manufacturer of upscale European cabinets, in the mid 1980s, and my relationship with the company quickly went from someone who represented its product in the United States to being part of the design team. I have designed four collections of cabinetry for SieMatic and among them is the Hudson Valley line, inspired by the butler's pantry, one of my favorite anterooms. It was used in a 2002 renovation of the Blair House, the president's guesthouse in Washington, D.C. My latest collection for SieMatic, named BeauxArts, speaks to my fondness for mixing.

BeauxArts is both modern and traditional. I designed the cabinetry (and other design elements like hoods and hardware) to be a sublime mix of vocabularies. That was the aesthetic goal. It allows the kitchen (and kitchen designer and client) to *not* be beholden to any one particular style. The simplicity allows client and designer to be free to imagine something new and different, to mix and let their dream for the kitchen dominate. The possibilities become endless

When I was a young designer in my twenties, I remember talking to Ken Nelson, who at the time was one of the chiefs of interior design at Ford. He was one of my clients; I had designed a kitchen for him and his wife, Audrey. In a lighthearted discussion about design, I said, half-jokingly, "I feel luckier than you, because I have a whole kitchen as my canvas. You only have the interior of a car. How many different ways can you really design the interior of a car?" Without pause, he said, "It's infinite." At that moment I realized how naive I was. Imagination is the only true limit to what we can create.

TENETS

Mick De Giulio

When I look at the kitchens in this book, I see my clients before anything else. Clients design their own kitchen, whether they know it or not. People feed me clues, and they may be as tangible as a photograph or as vague as a word or feeling. One client told me she wanted her kitchen to be breezy and elegant, like the feeling she had at Villa D'Este on Lake Como in Italy, where men dress up for breakfast. Another client showed me a bowl she bought in Positano, Italy. She loved the colors and the feel of it.

With that data and some measurements my design process begins, and it can be similarly amorphous. I do not believe in hard-and-fast rules (other than the law of function, because a kitchen has to work), just as I do not believe in following stylistic trends. The best kitchens defy labels and have their own personality and are beautiful no matter what the style.

What I do keep in my mind's eye are certain guiding principles—or tenets—of good design. Over the years, I have established seven of them, seven overriding ideas that I have found to be important to this process of creating something very special.

Space and Light

Light is what makes people feel alive, and it is what I think about first when designing a kitchen. Space gives the feeling of freedom and security. The goal in every kitchen—big or small, interior kitchen or one with giant windows—is to create feelings of openness and radiance and to promote what is already there.

I have a few favorite techniques: I look for every opportunity to gain even a few extra inches of natural light. I try not to put cabinets too close to windows, mindful of the importance of keeping the flow of natural light unrestricted. I also like to lower the height of windowsills to make them even or continuous with the countertop. The resulting view outside and the light streaming in feel so much bigger.

I like to float some of the massive components that are indigenous to kitchens. I may give an island legs to make it appear lighter and less obtrusive in the space. I also may design cabinets away from corners to give a sense of float. I rarely install any cabinets all the way up to the ceiling, which also allows for some nice uplighting. When the entire outline of a room (where the ceiling meets the wall) can be seen, the kitchen feels airier and the cabinets appear sculptural. Glass can create transparency and contribute to a spacious feeling as well. Clear or opaque glass-fronted doors on cabinets, sanded glass backsplashes and tabletops, and even (for the brave) glass-fronted refrigerators are possibilities.

This page, right photograph used with permission from *Beautiful Kitchens* magazine

Fresh and Clean

Fresh and clean are two timeless attributes especially pertinent to a space where food is prepared and served. Natural wood finishes have a brightness about them, and when combined with other elements that convey purity (such as stainless steel, glass, lighter-valued natural stones, and tiles), a lovely clarity can be achieved. Wall and paint finishes in lighter values with underlying tones of yellow and green also add to this sense of a fresh, clean space.

White is classic for kitchens. It will never be passé; it is irrepressibly fresh and pure. In the past, a white kitchen meant white cabinets, end of story. Now because people are more open to the idea of mixing, and because more elements have entered the picture, a predominantly white kitchen can have many different looks. Varying the shades of white within one kitchen gives depth and richness to all the white. I like playing with the variables—the walls, ceiling, floors, countertops— and making some or all of them white too. An all-white kitchen with white cabinets, white marble countertops, and limestone floors is fantastic. And the funny thing is the more you use white in a room, the less it feels like an element. The whiteness becomes dreamlike. Everything white sculpts together, which makes everything that is not white pop.

Function and Durability

A kitchen needs to work. That is the one hard-and-fast rule of good kitchen design. Each material, each object, each work zone must function extremely well, and the materials, in particular, must be durable. Hence, stainless steel is never out. It is practical (wipes clean, does not burn, scratches but I consider that patina), and it is beautiful. Stainless also is the consummate neutral and an exemplary mixer. It pairs beautifully with other materials.

Granite and many natural stones have similar attributes. And granite (often the favored choice because of its extraordinary durability) need not be the ubiquitous polished granite of the past. Granite can be honed to a matte finish or flamed to give it more texture and a more organic appearance. Mixing honed, flamed, and polished stone together in the same kitchen can be wonderful. Picture-framing elements of stone is another idea I use for countertops to make them more artful. For example, I may take a section of granite and surround it with a border of the same granite. The border is created by cutting narrow pieces of the stone and laminating them around the perimeter of the section with an opposing grain direction.

Although I am not against synthetic materials, if they are overdone, a space can end up looking flat and impersonal. Generally speaking, I am partial to natural materials such as wood and stone, although stainless is a man-made gem.

Mixing: Visual Texture and Counterpoints

I often use many types of woods, countertop materials, and finishes (not to mention design vocabularies) in one kitchen. I am often asked for the magic number: precisely how much mixing is right? The answer is simple: it is not about a number or mixing for the sake of mixing. It is about creating visual texture, and there is no right formula for that, but rather a right *feeling,* one kitchen at a time.

If a space is meant to look soft and the elements are mixed effectively, the mix looks effortless. A creamy/ochre and heavily veined granite might be used for an island countertop with a similarly toned French limestone on another countertop in the same kitchen. The effect is both warm and subtle.

And then there are mixes that create obvious drama, and they likely are based on counterpoints. I like to put man and machine in the same room—something with a strong hand-crafted quality and its counterpoint, something highly engineered like a velvet-brushed stainless steel refrigerator in a kitchen with hand-scraped maple floors. A hundred-year-old English book-case with splits in the wood is stunning among cabinets with a finish of high-gloss white lacquer. Color also can be mixed unex-pectedly—oxblood red and turquoise—as can formalities—a honed, Brazilian soapstone countertop juxtaposed with a polished Verde Antique Serpentine marble countertop. The whole idea is to create warmth, personality, mood.

Proportion and Scale

The right proportions give a kitchen rhythm and make it sing. Every single element needs to relate to the others and to the general space, and that includes everything from ceiling height and countertop thickness to door size.

To make a kitchen unique, standard proportions have to be challenged—changing what the mind and eye are accustomed to seeing. Countertop edges that are one-and-one-half-inches thick and refrigerators that are twenty-four to twenty-eight inches deep have been the standard in kitchens for decades, as have backsplashes that are sixteen to eighteen inches high.

Defying those norms, adding or subtracting from standard measures, sets the tone. I design countertops that range from three-eighths of an inch to six inches thick—and I often mix several thicknesses in a single kitchen. It is unlikely that anyone will pick up on the subtleties, but the kitchen will *feel* different.

I also like to de-mass the refrigerator by semi-recessing it into a wall so it appears to be eighteen inches or less in depth. Without that massive appliance immediately grabbing the eye, the kitchen feels more like a living space.

I like to de-mass cabinetry, too. I sometimes use wall cabinets sparingly or not at all to keep a kitchen open and airy. Or, I will semi-recess armoires. I like to break up a mass of base cabinets by constructing a frame around them. This changes the scale and heaviness of those base cabinets and places a pause between them and the countertop or a chunky professional appliance.

Opposite page: left photograph courtesy of SieMatic; this page: left photograph used with permission from *Traditional Home*® magazine

Composition Versus Continuum

Traditional kitchen design says cabinets run continuously and dominate a kitchen. I find a compositional approach more pleasing and artful. I break down a kitchen into various areas (perhaps a sink area, island, and wall section with ovens and refrigerator). And then I design each area as a composition, putting in the visual texture and considering various relationships among components.

I pay particular attention to range hoods. A custom-designed hood is a relatively small financial investment compared to the visual return it can provide. A unique hood creates an arful composition around the cooking area. And I pay particular attention to axial relationships—how the center of one element relates to the center of another. For instance, a focal point like an armoire or server might be aligned with an entry door. These axial relationships are more important than symmetry. They grace a space with a feeling of order and calm—and it happens quietly, subliminally.

Essence

I try to translate a special spirit or essence that comes from the client into the kitchen. Quirks are good. Personality is good. Both should be emphasized in a design, not diminished.

I do not think of a kitchen as architecture. Instead, I believe the kitchen can be the bond or link between people and the architecture of the house. Architecture and the kitchen do not have to match. Some of the most beautiful modern kitchens I have seen are in very old European houses and villas. The key is respecting the architecture in some way, and often that happens through proportion, scale, materials, and color.

A great kitchen personalizes the architecture. The kitchen should come alive in the house and provide a relief from the sometimes very serious architecture around it and reveal who the people are in a more personal way. Kitchens that have this wonderful human quality come from listening to people and turning their dreams into something functional and beautiful and unique.

18

KITCHENS

I. AIR

The house was to be French Provincial in style—9,000 square feet, stone, new construction. Above all else, it was not to feel contrived. The client, a woman of impeccable style and European sensibility marked by a particular fondness for France, was clear about that. She was overseeing the design and decoration, and she wanted her new family home to feel buoyant with light and air.

She envisioned the outdoors pouring in—and a kitchen with open arms and deep breaths. There would be an ivory stone floor (or some variation of it) paving the entire first floor, and it would remain natural (no polish) and bare (no rugs). There would be tall French doors all along the back of the house, including the area that would be the kitchen, which would encompass a family area and maybe a fireplace. She spoke of men dressing up for breakfast at Villa D'Este on Lake Como in Italy and her love for that feeling of freshness. She wanted it for her kitchen.

That was the briefing. Our operative words were clear: elegant, relaxed, modern, clean, airy. The kitchen would feel European, but nothing should be clichéd or too predictably French.

Originally, a dark island and blue-painted frames and muntins were specified for the French doors and windows, but later the color was replaced with a near-total whiteness, much of it matte. Minimal gloss. The look is sophisticated yet earthy. The pot rack offers the big dazzle, dangling like a piece of jewelry.

Throughout the space, point/counterpoint adds layers of richness—and surprise. The hand-carved limestone fireplace, for instance, looks thirty-six feet across the room at its alter ego—a simple, modern range hood. The black and stainless steel range wall is a foil for all the whiteness. The pine refrigerator/freezer armoire adds a complement of texture to a room that is otherwise smooth.

It also adds closed space in a kitchen that is brazenly exposed. The light and air needed an unobstructed course. An open island, open hutch, and iron plate rack take care of everyday storage with a disarming simplicity that comes from disclosing the contents of one's cabinets.

The openness also is a stage for the client's lovely style. The white wares, slipcovered furniture, and vintage chandelier were all hers. Along the top of the pine armoire, painted lightly, is an Italian saying: *ad ogni uccello il suo nido è bello.* To every bird, his nest is beautiful.

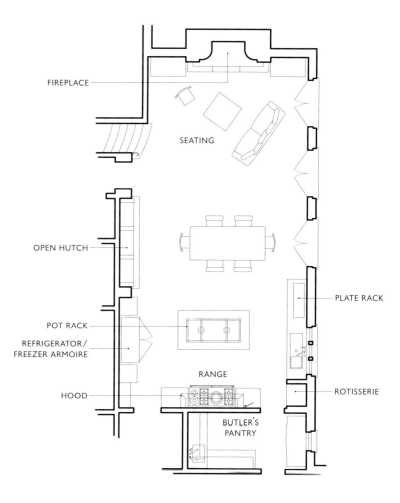

FIREPLACE

SEATING

OPEN HUTCH

PLATE RACK

POT RACK

REFRIGERATOR/
FREEZER ARMOIRE

RANGE

ROTISSERIE

HOOD

BUTLER'S
PANTRY

DINING ROOM

2. **SEEING BLUE**

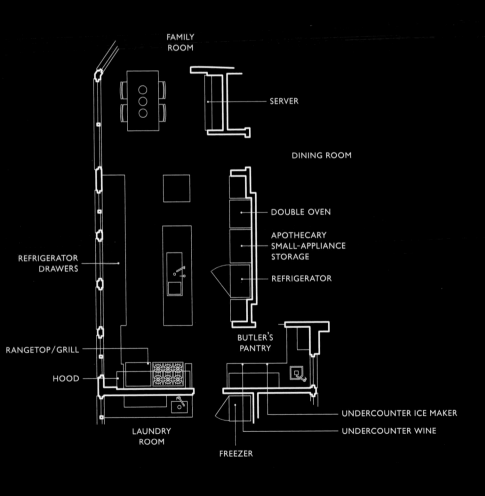

FAMILY
ROOM

SERVER

DINING ROOM

DOUBLE OVEN

APOTHECARY
SMALL-APPLIANCE
STORAGE

REFRIGERATOR

REFRIGERATOR
DRAWERS

RANGETOP/GRILL

HOOD

BUTLER'S
PANTRY

UNDERCOUNTER ICE MAKER

UNDERCOUNTER WINE

LAUNDRY
ROOM

FREEZER

WINNETKA, ILLINOIS

The kitchen was long and lean with an exterior wall that could have been spectacular. The would-be window wall had some windows in it, all right, but sadly, cabinets too. An ill-fated 1980s remodel left a mishmash of solid forms—cabinets and countertops jutting up and down, in and out, along with an island *and* a peninsula—that interrupted the sleekness of the rectangular space and made the whole room feel crowded and bloated. This kitchen was a diamond in the rough, a makeover waiting to happen.

The space would be nearly gutted (only the flooring remained) to clean the slate. We captured an additional six inches from the adjacent dining room, and that made all the difference. It allowed the island to be wide enough to include a sink, which suddenly directed anyone standing there into the kitchen. A similar epiphany happened at the exterior wall, the would-be spectacular wall. Out went the cabinets that were hanging there. In went a long stretch of windows. Now light came pouring in. A kitchen liberated.

The untangling and uncluttering would continue with the focus shifting to the other perimeter walls as well. In a long, narrow kitchen without a lot of open floor space, the drama can live in those defining walls, although they have to work double time, providing the support and the style.

Two ovens, the refrigerator, and a significant number of cabinets went into the wall facing the windows. What could have been a jumble of shapes was tempered and equalized by doing (nearly) the whole thing in stainless steel. That silvery wall then became a framework for an ebonized walnut apothecary, which adds a counterpoint of texture and darkness (and houses a microwave and other small appliances). To the side, the range wall continues to define the clean rectangle with a strong, modern composition.

The island was not a problem. Given the length of the kitchen and the inconvenience of having to walk around one very long island, it made sense to divide it into two, albeit not equal, parts.

The small walnut island (for linens) with the countertop in blue is the kitchen's grand gesture, done in one quick exclamation point. The space demanded restraint. The countertop material is *cottopesto*, a terra-cotta that is fired, colored, and shaped into custom forms by artisans in Italy. It is a work of abstract art with the addition of molten aluminum, which inserted little silver gems into the surface. Red was the obvious color for that *cottopesto* with all the warm, reddish tones in both the flooring and dark cabinets. So we chose blue.

3. **COLLECTED**

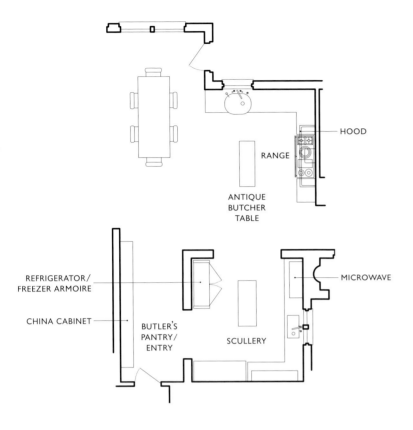

HOOD

RANGE

ANTIQUE
BUTCHER
TABLE

REFRIGERATOR/
FREEZER ARMOIRE

MICROWAVE

CHINA CABINET

BUTLER'S
PANTRY/
ENTRY

SCULLERY

They had been collecting their Provençal dream house for years. French country furniture and English antiques, windows, doors, roof and floor tiles, columns, and even sacks of plaster—they had it all, assembled over their years of travels to Europe, shipped back to the United States and kept in quiet storage. There were culinary antiques, too, most found in their hometown of New Orleans, also lying in wait.

The clients had a French farmhouse on their minds and soon it would be on their land. The ground had been broken at last. They wanted this farmhouse to be authentic—simple, warm, earthy, as if it had been cobbled together over generations. The kitchen would follow suit. It would be built around the antique cabinets in their stash but be modern in function and include a modern French range.

We deemed the range yellow for no reason other than it seemed right. It gave rise to the dramatic hood, one of the kitchen's most significant elements. The hood was designed to look as though it had been there for two hundred years—or made yesterday. Its clean lines did well to blur the provenance of the piece. Copper or wood would have been obvious material choices but would have made the hood gargantuan. So instead, we opted for plaster. Visually, that giant hood melts into the back wall.

But it's essential. The hood straddles the divide between old and new in this kitchen and holds everything together. Unlike most projects, this one was not a blank canvas. The client's beloved antiques were a critical part of the design program. The new was beholden to the old, the old needed some reinvention, and all of that had to get along in a union that was to be warm and humble. Super slick was not the goal.

And so, the hand-carved oblong travertine sink from Italy doesn't fit perfectly into the square cabinet—by design.

And refrigeration doesn't live in the optimal place—by choice. (It lives in the adjacent scullery, inside a pine armoire.) The clients rejected the idea of an island with built-in refrigerator drawers, positioned near the range. They wanted their own antique butcher block table there and were willing to walk a few steps out of their way to access cold storage. They were willing to walk for the microwave and coffeemaker, too. These appliances are located in the scullery as well. The clients liked the idea of tucking the every-day, working part of the kitchen out of sight, away from the cooking theater.

Staying simple and choosing good materials that patinate well were important to the union of new and old, thus the Scoon (a durable French limestone) and lavastone countertops, and the travertine sink. The new butternut wood cabinets were key, too. Butternut takes on a beautiful burnished quality in a rigorous finishing process that includes stain, glaze, and hand-scraping.

Another secret to the union: negative space. A modern structure (a thin coat of Venetian plaster over wood) frames some of the base cabinets, including those adjoining the range, yielding pause between the counter and the deeply wooded cabinets. It also changes the scale of the base cabinets in an interesting way, teaching the old (or made to look old) cabinets a modern trick—breathing room.

Where we cannot invent, we may at least improve; we may give somewhat of novelty to that which was old.

—CHARLES C. COLTON (1780–1832)

4. **HANDSOME**

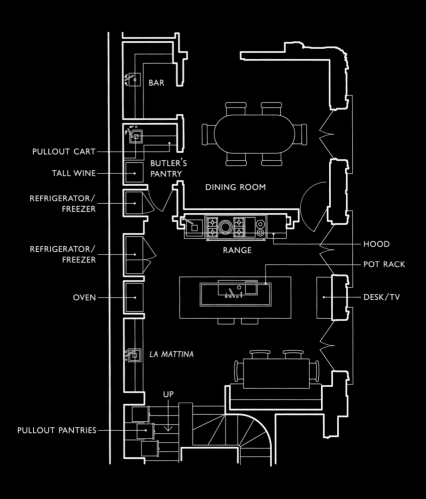

PULLOUT CART

TALL WINE

REFRIGERATOR/
FREEZER

REFRIGERATOR/
FREEZER

OVEN

PULLOUT PANTRIES

BAR

BUTLER'S
PANTRY

DINING ROOM

RANGE

LA MATTINA

UP

HOOD

POT RACK

DESK/TV

CHICAGO, ILLINOIS

The man of the house was in charge of the family's kitchen project and he was clear about wanting a French bistro flavor. I, on the other hand, was not entirely clear what that should mean, given the context of this house and this particular client.

He is a sophisticated businessman with definite preferences and a leader, never a follower. The house, located in Chicago's Gold Coast, likewise conveys authority. At a width of merely twenty-four feet, the stone house (circa 2008) strikes a commanding presence with its French neoclassical good looks.

We all knew that reproducing the classic bistro look (think lots of black-and-white tile flooring and heavy on the drapery) would be predictable and wrong, but it led us to the idea of creating something more Parisian modern. The kitchen would have a French feeling and just a moment of black-and-white tile, which we pulled off with great effect in the butler's pantry. But overall, the tone would be stronger, more masculine, more streamlined.

Our palette of materials — white marble, dark wenge wood in a high-gloss finish, stainless steel, nickel silver — struck the right classic-handsome note. The gloss in the wenge, stainless, and nickel (along with the reflective quality of the glass cabinets) adds sophistication and plays nicely against the ruggedness of the hand-scraped maple floors. The weighty, French range and commercial-looking refrigerator also lend a masculine feel, as does the custom-made, stainless steel rolling ladder.

Like the house itself, the kitchen is long, lean, and vertical. The ceiling climbs at least fourteen feet, which was both asset and challenge. The height allowed us to do a double-stack of upper cabinets, which is something I usually avoid, because the top row is unreachable. But in this case, it got us critical storage space for items not used daily and a lowering effect for that distant ceiling. We added coffers to the ceiling for texture and for acoustic purposes and, again, to rein in the vastness. The three-inch-wide, square-edged marble countertop on the island further grounds the space.

Height was not the only dimension that mattered. The length of the space needed tempering too, which is why I did not design one continuous run of cabinetry for the long wall. Instead, I sectioned that wall into three compositions of varying size and rhythm — the morning area (la mattina) with its own sink and dishwasher, the oven, and the refrigeration.

This compositional approach also enabled us to create axial relationships with other key parts of the room. Axial relationships give a subtle sense of calmness and order to a space without necessarily having to be symmetrical or perfect about it. The oven, for instance, is centered with the island; the island is centered with the desk/TV. So these two opposing elements — the oven and TV, which are almost the same size but not exactly — share a center-line and address each other from across the room.

Beyond the banquette, up a flight of steps leading to a family space, we had one final triumph — more critical storage. We inserted (shoehorned, actually) three long, pullout pantries into the hollow wall next to that staircase, in staggered rhythm with the steps.

This is a kitchen that works hard and has a chef's sensibility — but it has no overdone theme. Instead, we strove to give this classic French *maison* a handsome elegance.

5. **FEARLESS**

Photograph by Julian Wass for House Beautiful magazine, 2009

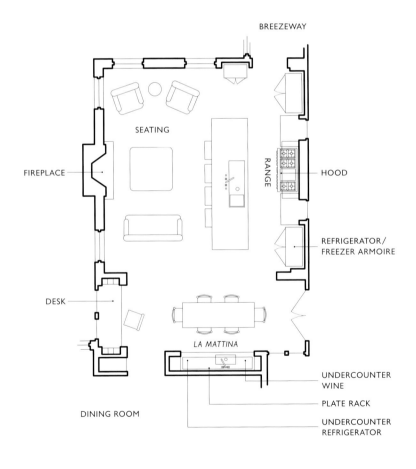

BREEZEWAY

SEATING

FIREPLACE

RANGE

HOOD

REFRIGERATOR/
FREEZER ARMOIRE

DESK

LA MATTINA

UNDERCOUNTER
WINE

PLATE RACK

UNDERCOUNTER
REFRIGERATOR

DINING ROOM

Photograph by Julian Wass for House Beautiful magazine, 2009

GLENCOE, ILLINOIS

It takes self-awareness to know exactly what one wants and courage to persevere, especially when the object of one's desire is unconventional.

From the start, the client had this idea of a white kitchen, a kitchen so very white that it would become dreamlike. She was convinced it would have a dark wood floor and thought perhaps a limited number of other dark elements, but the aura of the room would be ethereal. The cabinets, countertops, backsplashes, trim, walls, ceiling had to be snow white. She would carry that whiteness throughout the rest of her home, a 1950s Cape Cod that was in the midst of a gut renovation and already in the framing stage when we were called in to design the kitchen.

My staff and I immediately got excited about a space that would be so simple it would be complex, and anything but boring. We were not so excited about something more immediately pressing—the kitchen's location.

The kitchen had been assigned a spot at the back of the house, far from the garage (inconvenient for toting groceries) and too far from the family living space (inconvenient for family togetherness for this family with two young children). And where it stood in the floor plan, the kitchen had no room to grow a living area.

The client came to agree and the kitchen took its more rightful spot in the front of the house, which also gave the kitchen a soaring ceiling and more square footage to incorporate family space, complete with a fireplace and ample comfy seats.

With the geography matter settled, we dove into the plan and into further bravery. Simple is often a hard sell, but not with this client. She led the charge for just one color and utter simplicity. Accordingly, we avoided curves and flourishes and opted instead for strong rectilinear shapes throughout. To keep things dreamy, we created open areas above the cabinets to let the space breathe. We also de-massed the larger, rectilinear forms (the refrigerator/freezer and pantry, both flanking the range) by building out the range wall and tucking those elements into that wall.

We played with thicks and thins and added slivers of darkness to create texture and counterpoint. The delicate chandelier, for instance, lives in contrast to the solidness of the cabinetry and the massive feeling of the deeply set windows along the range wall, a result of the wall being built out. The dark wood flooring, farm table and chairs, and counter stools ground the whiteness and keep it from floating away visually without interrupting the quiet as does the counterpoint of dark limestone counters along the range wall.

The strongest visual pun, though, is the triple-bayed, polished nickel plate rack in the *la mattina* (morning) area. Although the piece is visually light, it strikes a commanding presence and steals the eye when entering the kitchen from the white breezeway that is a gallery of light and the passage to the garage.

Without a doubt, the pièce de résistance in this kitchen is the play of light. The rectilinear forms slice the natural light into shards and shadows—a complex web of simplicity. And under the soaring canopy of light, the kitchen's brave starkness turns into pure glow.

All photographs on this spread by Julian Wass for *House Beautiful* magazine, 2009

Jonathan West for House Beautiful magazine, 2009

Those who dream by day are cognizant of many things which escape those who dream only by night.

— **EDGAR ALLAN POE** (1809–1849) *Eleanora*

6. **NO PROBLEM**

CHICAGO, ILLINOIS

A location on the sixty-second floor of a downtown building with fabulous light and views of the city—all something of a tease for this condo kitchen, which existed as an interior room. It had no windows, no view, no profound natural light, no fabulousness whatsoever.

Our charge (part of a larger remodel) was to make something wonderful out of that kitchen, a room claimed by the man of the house. He likes to cook, and along with his wife, they envisioned doing some serious entertaining there.

The usual, sticky points of a high-rise (adding recessed ceiling lights, venting) were not trivial, but the most salient issue was figuring out how to bring better attributes to that kitchen. We did it by enlarging the opening between the kitchen and dining room, making that passage twelve feet wide. Suddenly, the kitchen had daylight and a skyline view. Working with the clients' architect and interior designer, we added pocket doors so the kitchen could be closed off at a whim.

With the kitchen now breathing, we worked on the layout, keeping in mind that this was to be an entertaining space, and space was limited. The island emerged as the linchpin of the plan; we made the decision to put the cooktop in it. Now the kitchen had an outward focus. The clients could be cooking at the island and facing their guests, gathered around. (We kept counter stools out of the equation, and the space open by creating a small eating area adjacent to the island.) But this decision also got us into trouble. It meant we had to place the range hood in the center of the kitchen. The last thing we wanted was a blocky obstruction to the new light and views.

I designed that hood to be as thin as possible by giving it a faceted profile and knifelike edge with each corner angled to promote sightlines. Stainless steel augments the sense of lightness; halogens inserted inside boost the downlight.

The aesthetic plan happened more easily. The kitchen wanted to be sleek like the rest of the apartment. To create a seamlessness, we again collaborated with the clients' architect and interior designer and used the same Santos rosewood African mahogany for much of the cabinetry, with material cut from the same trees as the rest of the apartment. We used the same wood plank flooring chosen for the rest of the apartment, as well. To that we added stainless steel—ever slick and the consummate neutral—and sanded glass (sink backsplash and breakfast tabletop) for its translucency. The island got an Ivory Chiffon granite top, which is a story unto itself.

We wanted the modernity of chalky limestone, except, unfortunately, the lighter limestones can be soft and show wear and tear. So instead, we opted for this relatively inexpensive granite—and played with it, trying to transform it into something unlike granite. After a number of experiments, our Italian fabricator delivered the undulating, glossless finish we were after, using a diamond-brush technique. We were later told it was one of the first attempts at brushing granite.

A final caveat is the pantry area, carved out of a corridor with a low ceiling. We lined the space with storage cabinets and fronted them with sanded glass to keep the space airy. The tracks of recessed ceiling light look chic but were actually dire solutions. An air-conditioning vent claimed the center of the ceiling space; recessed cans were not an option.

And that is what I like most about this kitchen. Challenges became inspiration.

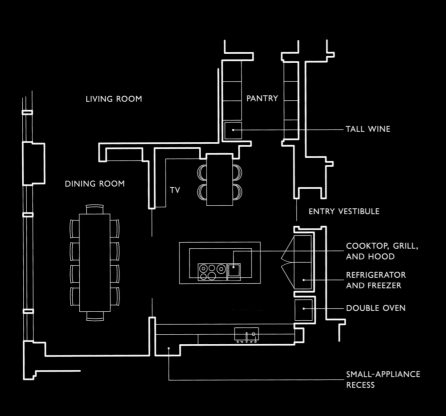

LIVING ROOM

PANTRY

TALL WINE

DINING ROOM

TV

ENTRY VESTIBULE

COOKTOP, GRILL, AND HOOD

REFRIGERATOR AND FREEZER

DOUBLE OVEN

SMALL-APPLIANCE RECESS

We are continually faced with a series of great opportunities brilliantly disguised as insoluble problems.

—**JOHN W. GARDNER** (1912–2002)

7. **HORSEPOWER**

The old gray boards were not going away. Nor were the horse stalls, or the urine trough.

The owners of the early twentieth-century barn were excited about converting it into a guesthouse but adamant about salvaging the integrity of the rustic structure, which existed as an outbuilding on their property. The plan called for filling the barn with a soaring living room, one loft bedroom, one and one-half baths, and a kitchen suitable for a couple of guests or a full-fledged party. There would be no walls added, save for some rejiggering in the baths. Their only concession—hiring an artist to refurbish the original wood.

The kitchen landed in the nitty-gritty of what used to be the horse living quarters. Three stalls, three feed bins, and a urine trough occupied one side of the large space. And on the other side were a lone structural column and a novel, but difficult, Dutch door that swung open to the outside.

The Party Barn (as it affectionately came to be known) was born to be a rebel. Creating the right look and feel—the optimal mix of warmth and rawness—became the mission. Making the kitchen functional would be the trick.

The ball got rolling with the addition of a second column, a pseudo-mate for the off-center structural one that existed in the more open part of the room. We opted to insert an island between the two columns and hung a pot rack overhead. Suddenly, there was order and logic.

But it would not, could not last. Instead of placing the expected single sink between the two windows under the Dutch door, we decided two sinks should be installed, one under each window. This decision jibed with the kitchen's offbeat personality but also made sense for multiple cooks. A cabinet then was built in front of the Dutch door, which allowed for a continuous worktop area between the two sinks and turned the curious door into a functional pass-through for serving meals outdoors.

Across the kitchen proper lived the former horse stalls—and the seeming absurdity of having three small, partitioned spaces in a would-be kitchen. The mantra "Party Barn" helped loosen the imagination. This could get a bit wild.

And so, the stall space was designated an auxiliary area, to be invoked during large-scale entertaining. Each stall would have its own function. There would be the storage stall, equipped with a hutch; the cooking stall, with an oven that sits behind louvered swing doors; and the cleanup stall, with a dishwasher and nickel silver sink.

Traditional barn vocabulary influenced a number of design decisions but was not allowed to get cute. The nickel silver pot rack, for instance, is in the shape of a half-wagon wheel. The refrigerator/freezer is housed inside a cabinet designed to look like a modern icebox (which we semi-recessed into the wall so it looks less like a major appliance). The range hood is a nonliteral interpretation of a traditional barrel shape.

Because the interior of the barn is covered in old wooden boards, a vast grayness prevails, and it had to be reckoned with—and reconciled. Teak was the wood choice for most of the new cabinets. It fades and mellows from its reddish color over time, with light.

But the grayness could not roll on and on in overpowering severity. An infusion of warm woods (butternut, maple) with strong shots of nickel silver and stainless steel toned down the bleakness and made the space feel raw and modern, but also genuinely warm—for guests of the two-legged variety.

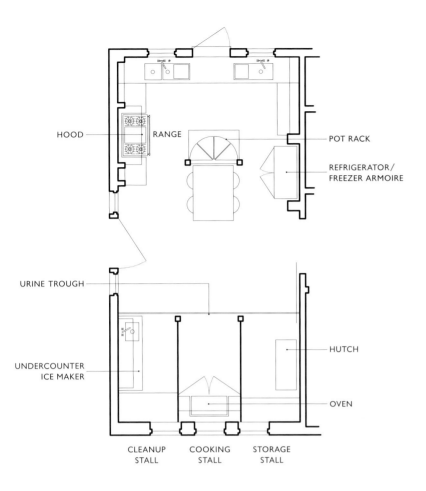

HOOD — RANGE

POT RACK

REFRIGERATOR/
FREEZER ARMOIRE

URINE TROUGH

HUTCH

UNDERCOUNTER
ICE MAKER

OVEN

CLEANUP
STALL

COOKING
STALL

STORAGE
STALL

8. **RETREAT**

Not every kitchen is born to be conspicuous. Some kitchens are designed to be backdrops that simply engender an impression of beauty.

The owners of this urban pied-à-terre wanted their loft apartment to be a sophisticated but serene setting for their beautiful objects, which include Japanese art and artifacts. The kitchen must not break the overall understatement of the apartment. It had to flow seamlessly into the rest of the open loft and be barely noticeable. This meant we had to make the telltale signs that say "kitchen" (cabinets, refrigerator, range) either disappear or be very quiet. And we had the same issue with the unfortunate structural column that landed prominently in the kitchen proper.

We took our cue from the Japanese sense of simplicity and established a palette of materials and colors in earthy modern—Bavarian white oak, stone (both a light-colored granite and a terra-cotta colored French limestone), and ribbed aluminum laminate cabinets. The cabinets are finished with the look of raw driftwood. The delicate texture from the ribbing and the oak graining give the kitchen movement.

There are no wall cabinets in direct view from the living space. We chose a panel of back-sanded glass for the range backsplash for its spare quality. It looks like a wall of still water and the plaster hood, like a fold of origami. Throughout, we were conscious of balance, contrasting strict shapes with organic ones, raw finishes with polished materials.

There is one set of wall cabinets to the side of the kitchen, out of plain view, where there is also a notable appliance garage that we recessed into the wall, gave oak doors, and made automatic. With sanded glass fronts and thin metal frames, the cabinets in this area appear to float above the oak countertop and below a trio of open display shelves for artwork. Behind those cabinets, beyond a simple unframed sanded glass door, is the walk-in pantry.

While the Japanese aesthetic dominates, this kitchen gives a nod to Paris via the handcrafted French range. Its detailing in nickel and black enamel offers a counterpoint to the simple, sleek, framed cabinets flanking it.

As for that awkward structural column, we called upon both aesthetics—European and Asian—to turn it into a quiet but formidable component. We clad the column in oak, detailed the countertop around it, and graced it with oak shelves sans any visible hardware. A second columnar form was added along the kitchen's back wall, and it offers visual balance to the open-walled area of the range. We recessed the refrigerator/freezer into that white column, and it henceforth ceased to be a major mass of appliance. It is, instead, a simple block of silver.

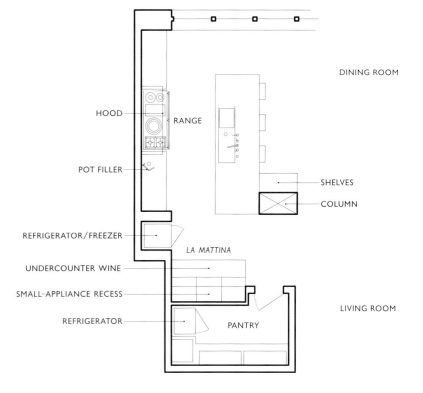

DINING ROOM

HOOD

RANGE

POT FILLER

SHELVES

COLUMN

REFRIGERATOR/FREEZER

LA MATTINA

UNDERCOUNTER WINE

SMALL-APPLIANCE RECESS

REFRIGERATOR

PANTRY

LIVING ROOM

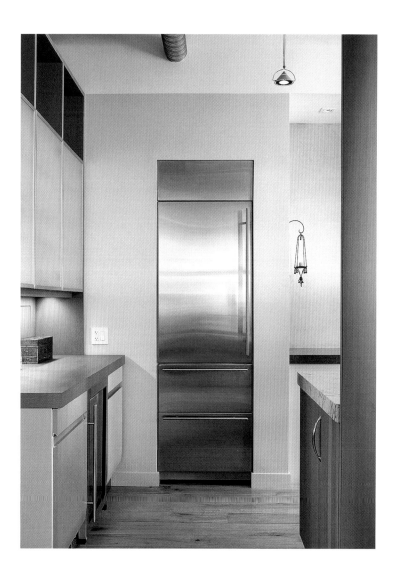

9. **SIDE SHOW**

LONG ISLAND, NEW YORK

The house on the bay reminds me of Thomas Jefferson's famous Monticello, not only because of the wood floors and painted woodwork, but for its uncannily pleasing proportions. The house is large and magnificent, but livable; you feel important in this place. The question was how to make the open (and relatively small) kitchen feel important in the grand family living space that adjoins it, where a barrel-vaulted ceiling and array of tall windows on the back of the house steal the show with a view of the bay.

We were called in to answer that question when the house was still under construction, and the kitchen was nothing more than square footage. It was clear to me, though, that this square footage did not want to be a dutiful, traditional kitchen. Here was a kitchen destined to assert itself and claim its own personality. The family space, which felt like a grand hall, was too strong for any one piece of it to be coy.

The first challenge was figuring out how to handle that transition from grand theater to side stage—from barrel-vaulted living space to adjacent kitchen—when the entire space was open and connected. We accomplished that shift by giving the kitchen definition and something of a marquee, namely a long work island of ebonized walnut and light marble. The island acts as a sentry to the kitchen space and announces the kitchen's significance. It also gives the cook an outward view to the family space and beyond, to the bay.

We spent a lot of time detailing that island, because of its prominence. We gave it legs (even though it houses the dishwasher and cabinets) to make it look like a piece of furniture and integrated its sink into the marble worktop, again to be sensitive to the living area beyond. The real sleight of hand is in the polished stainless steel shroud at the base edge of the island. That piece hides the plumbing and dishwasher and performs beautiful tricks with the light; the stainless steel reflects the floor and gives a sense of float to this large island.

Throughout, we opted for a palette of dark walnut and light marble because it is classic like the house, but also because it can be simple and modern, especially when interrupted with moments of gloss, like those provided by the stainless steel appliances and one bank of high-gloss ebonized walnut base cabinets in a side counter/storage area. The client was hesitant about glossing up the walnut, thinking it would look too contemporary. We came to an interesting resolution by pairing those base cabinets with glass-fronted uppers done in nickel silver, a beautiful old material that brings a streamlined glamour. The backsplash is done in the same nickel silver (but with mirror insets), and it is motorized, making it easy to stash small appliances and keep the kitchen looking uncluttered.

The Italian sanded glass tile on the range wall is more resolutely contemporary, as is the stainless steel range hood. We chose those glass tiles for their liquid quality; the glass seems to pull the water view in from the other side of the room. A butler's pantry adjoining the main kitchen completes the space and hides kitchen essentials. Open shelving gives an airy tone. The classic-looking base cabinets are in an elegant gray-green that is almost white but has a character of its own.

And that is what we were striving for here—a kitchen with a character of its own, on an intrepid side stage.

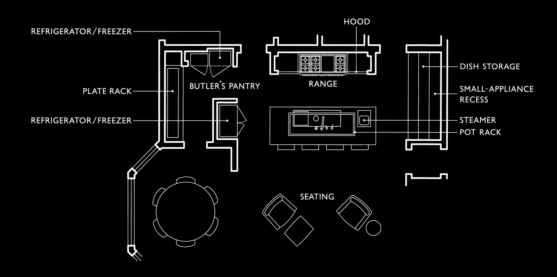

10. **BOOM**

It is not often that one has the opportunity to design a lightning bolt and hang it horizontally across a room in the form of a continuous, nearly eighteen-foot-long streak of stainless steel.

Perhaps one of our most streamlined designs, this kitchen lives inside a 1990s modern house that the clients had purchased from the original owners, notable Chicago art collectors. Those owners had commissioned a prominent London-based architect to design them a gallerylike dwelling, and indeed, the house is an impeccable specimen of less-is-more—an exalted composition of space and light.

We were called in to redo the kitchen, which had seen some wear and needed to be more family-friendly. We replaced the existing island with a larger one that has lower cabinet space easily accessible for children and added a custom-made display cabinet (near the kitchen table) specifically designed to hold the family's beloved painting on good table manners.

But with the kids now attended to, this was a kitchen that also had to be bold. The existing modern aesthetic reigned hard and supreme, with the axes and lines palpable in the space. The back wall gridded with oversize ceramic tiles (which we all liked far too much to remove) was barely there, yet enormous. Entering through a large skylight in a single stack of whiteness, the light felt almost sacred. Interestingly, there are no traditional windows. The kitchen has two sets of glass and metal doors on either side of the space, leading to two small enclosed atrium rooms. It is that giant light well over the working part of the kitchen that brings most of the light in during the day. It was clear we could not be demure.

We chose a palette of colors and materials that could convey both strong and soft. Stainless steel had to be in, in a big way, in both the details and key elements. We chose the silvery metal because it epitomizes edgy and strong and yet remains visually light. To that slickness, we added the organic counterpoint: light oak for the cabinets and green Costa Smeralda honed granite for the island countertop. Both the grainy oak and honed stone offer texture and a clear, but measured warmth—a warmth that does not interfere with the space and light.

It is the stainless steel, though, that prevails in our design. We used it to answer the modern call and to raise it a notch or two, most notably in that shelf along the back wall, which became the kitchen's focal point. A utensil/pot rail existed here before, but it looked tired and visually flimsy. The shelf (which was crafted in one piece and has cold cathode lighting embedded in the top and bottom for both task and effect lighting) brings a bolt of modernity, at once silvery, lean, and powerful to the kitchen and sharpens the glorious horizontality that already existed. It also freshens and renews the modern spirit here, enhancing its effect for the next generation.

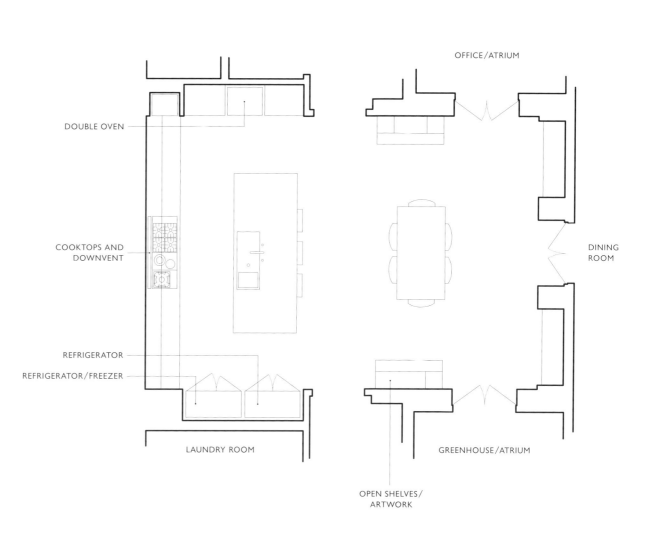

OFFICE/ATRIUM

DOUBLE OVEN

COOKTOPS AND
DOWNVENT

DINING
ROOM

REFRIGERATOR

REFRIGERATOR/FREEZER

LAUNDRY ROOM

GREENHOUSE/ATRIUM

OPEN SHELVES/
ARTWORK

II. POP

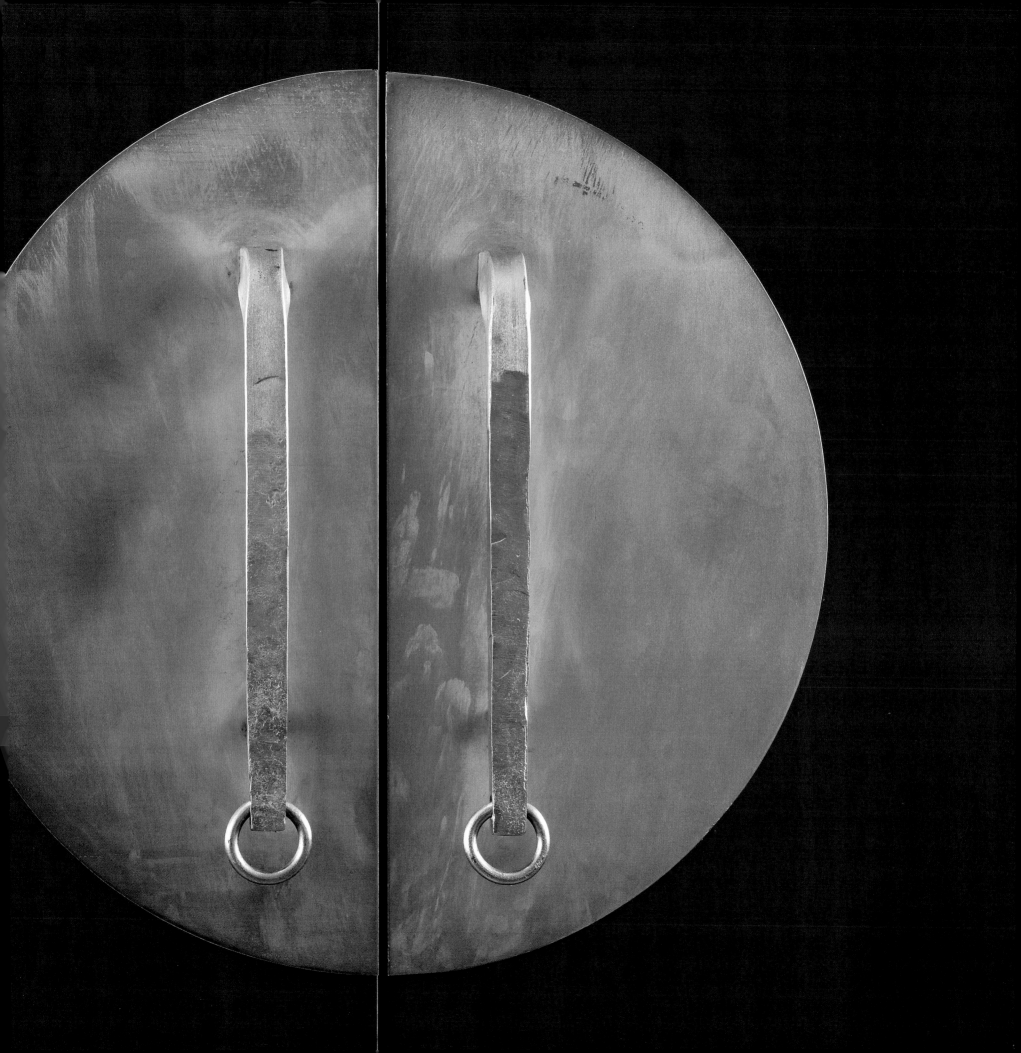

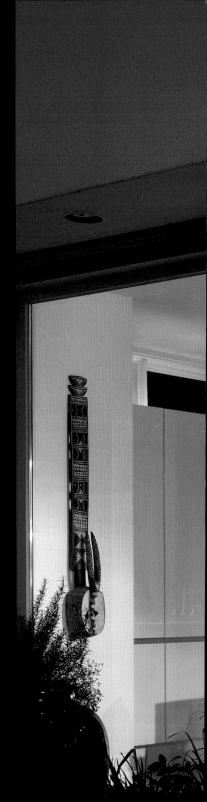

WINNETKA, ILLINOIS

The kitchen needed space, storage, and a *do-no-harm* clause. Recently married, the clients had purchased a modern home for their large, blended family. A renovation was underway, and it included the kitchen, which needed updating to accommodate this new family of fourteen.

Our mandate: more cabinet space, more stashing places, improved efficiency, *and more room.* We took advantage of the high clerestory on the side elevation and loaded that wall with cabinets. On the facing wall went a long desk area and a separate breakfast/cleanup station, both laden with storage. A wine bar was built into a vestibule that leads to the dining room. And the island became filled with places to stash cooking equipment, books, and papers.

But something about this kitchen could not be captured on paper, in the space planning—namely, the spectacular view of the backyard and pool area, seen through the kitchen's back wall of glass. The house's original architect clearly delivered that outward focus and we needed to honor and protect it even if it would be infringed upon. The clients decided to extend that back wall into the yard by about four feet to increase the space in the eating area. They consulted the original architect to keep the architecture pure.

Still, we took our role as protectionists seriously and designed an aesthetic plan to ensure that the view remained the focus. That plan also jibed with the clients' personal style. They are avid travelers and collectors of art, particularly from the East. They like their homes to be open, spacious, quiet places—getaways from the world outside and backdrops for their collections. A clean look suited them and answered the call for a kitchen that would serve as a smooth conduit, gliding the eye through the space and setting it outward bound, to the enclosed yard.

We bathed the kitchen in high-gloss white cabinets (devoid of detail, including hardware), stainless steel, warm gray granite, and sanded glass. The lighting design made minimal the essence, as well. We installed a constellation of recessed cans without trims, and for a seamless effect, we had the ceiling painted in the same textured linen finish that envelops the room.

The kitchen reads as utter smoothness—save for one necessary burst of exuberance and a couple of supporting ripples. We interrupted the continuum with a hand-painted armoire in a Chinese red lacquer finish that holds the refrigerator and freezer. For the color and aged finish, I was inspired by an antique lacquer table that my wife and I have in our house; I took one of the drawers to an artist and asked him to replicate that striated red on a new piece of cabinetry that we had built using unfinished but primed wood.

The burst of color is a welcome relief to all the white lacquer, giving the eye something bold yet serene to land on, gently. The knotty maple

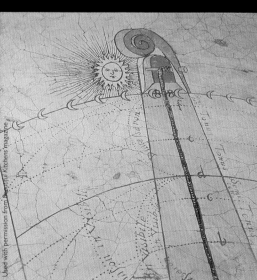

POOL

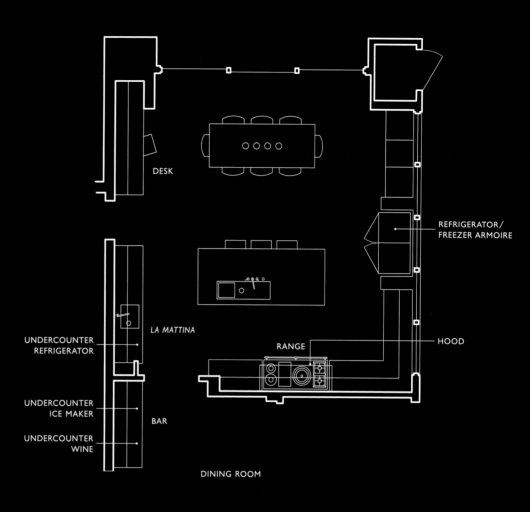

DESK

REFRIGERATOR/
FREEZER ARMOIRE

LA MATTINA

UNDERCOUNTER
REFRIGERATOR

RANGE

HOOD

UNDERCOUNTER
ICE MAKER

BAR

UNDERCOUNTER
WINE

DINING ROOM

12. **MELLOW DRAMA**

ATHERTON, CALIFORNIA

The house has a tower and enough chimneys to be a backdrop in a Hollywood movie, which is fitting. The owners like to cultivate the drama in their rooms and spaces and make their home feel comfortable and vibrant. They had purchased this French Normandy house, built in 1928, and were set to renovate with panache.

As part of my education, the young couple showed me the home where they were still living with their three children when they called me into the project—to learn who they are, how they live, how they like living with art, and what they did (and did not) want to incorporate into their new life in their quirky new-old house.

Quirky was key. The clients love the element of surprise. Their former home (a newer, more contemporary house) was filled with a mix of antiques, modern furniture, and a bold collection of mostly contemporary artwork that made the sum-total-house funky, in a good way.

And so, when the couple asked for a kitchen that was "different," I interpreted that as a mandate to create a mix of artful components that somehow work together, possibly pushing, but not offending, the Normandy.

Mix was another key word here, and always is in my kitchens, but it would take on special significance in this project. We would arrive at "different" by keeping that mantra of "artful" in our heads, and then stir things up with our mixes of materials, colors, and contrasts of traditional with modern.

The ebonized walnut cabinets adjacent to the range (in an area that includes a recess for housing small appliances) are English-looking and traditional. We intentionally played them between two modern elements: the apothecary cabinet (also ebonized walnut) that houses the refrigerator/freezer and the sleek stainless steel cabinets that flank the range. The quiet white marble island sits in bold contrast to its red leather counter stools and to the adjacent dark walnut linen table with a colorful mosaic top.

We mined our artfulness in elements such as that mosaic countertop; the Murano glass pendant lamps; the steely range hood, which has an aura of modern art; and the dramatic range wall of marble, whose veining is downright painterly. The custom-painted glass tiles (a technique called *eglomise*) in the morning area (*la mattina*) add a splash of unexpected pattern, which was inspired by a whimsically ornate Italian fabric. Open shelves done in a framework of polished nickel hang from that *eglomise* tile wall. Below are cabinets faced in nickel silver.

The kitchen flows with no interruption into a family space, where the ceiling jumps to eighteen feet, a new addition to the house along with a portion of the kitchen space. The dark wood beams also designed by the clients' architect bring that tall ceiling down and smooth the transition between spaces. And they, along with the ebonized walnut cabinet I designed to house the TV, nod to the kitchen and its dark components. The two columnlike cabinets flanking the entry to the sitting bay also do some nodding—to the funky side. I designed them with carved feet and a linen fold detail, a combination of English manor and French classic styling that wound up looking modern.

Clearly this is not the kitchen one would expect of a French Normandy house. The finishes and materials were chosen to be artful characters that at once bow to this vintage masterpiece and tug at it a bit, taking it to places modern.

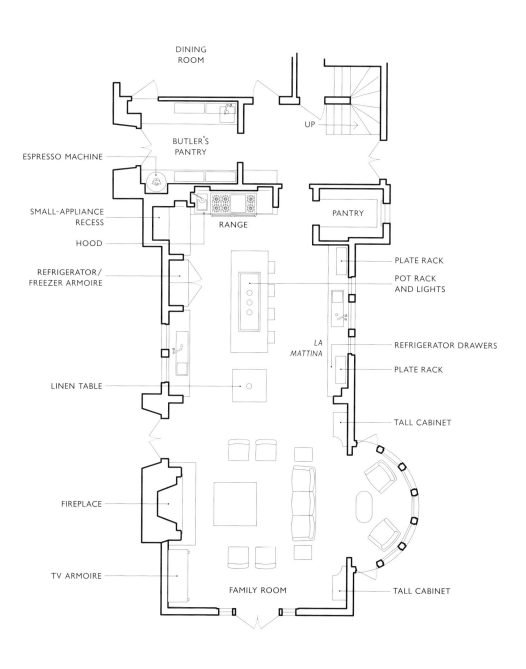

DINING
ROOM

BUTLER'S
PANTRY

UP

ESPRESSO MACHINE

PANTRY

SMALL-APPLIANCE
RECESS

RANGE

HOOD

PLATE RACK

REFRIGERATOR/
FREEZER ARMOIRE

POT RACK
AND LIGHTS

LA
MATTINA

REFRIGERATOR DRAWERS

PLATE RACK

LINEN TABLE

TALL CABINET

FIREPLACE

TV ARMOIRE

FAMILY ROOM

TALL CABINET

Drama is life with the dull bits cut out.

— **ALFRED HITCHCOCK** (1899–1980)

13. **RESTRAINT**

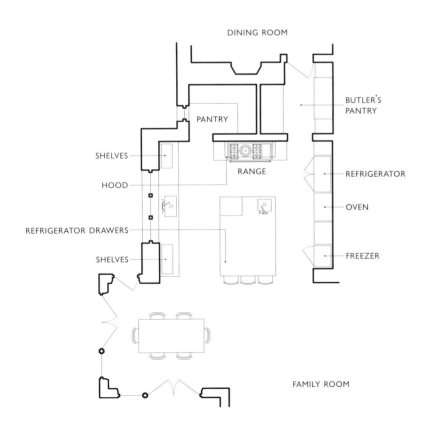

DINING ROOM

BUTLER'S
PANTRY

PANTRY

SHELVES

RANGE

HOOD

REFRIGERATOR

OVEN

REFRIGERATOR DRAWERS

SHELVES

FREEZER

FAMILY ROOM

One of the secrets of good design is knowing when to stop designing.

The clients understood this well before we stepped into the picture. Inspired by their honeymoon in the south of France a decade prior, they had built a Provençal farmhouse. They wanted it to be authentic, which involved making about eight trips to Europe to hunt up everything from wooden beams and fireplaces to stone and tile. But never did they lose sight of their farmhouse goal. They resisted the temptation to overdo the place.

They kept the architecture and details simple (no heavy molding or ornamentation), just as a country house would be. And so, when they called us in to deliver a kitchen, there was no good reason to go overboard with the French vocabulary and every good reason to stay simple and clean.

Their vision for the kitchen already included a stone wall and exposed timber beams, and probably the chevron-patterned wood floor and the steel and glass doors, too. That was strong enough on the European theme. The kitchen didn't need and, perhaps couldn't stand, a heavily tiled backsplash or imposing range hood. Many old European farmhouses added their kitchens in later years, so it is not uncommon for a true farmhouse kitchen to break aesthetically from the rest of the house and look more modern.

Instead of invoking old Europe, we turned to the house's rustic modernity and again found answers in that mantra of simple and clean. The clients took a leap of faith and said yes to our call for a stainless steel range hood and sanded glass backsplash on the range wall, which sound too contemporary. But they look spare and understated and exactly right against the timber and stone—and the white marble countertops and ebonized walnut cabinets.

That tried-and-true, light marble/dark wood combination worked beautifully here because it is such a classic and such a chameleon. By inserting a light-colored structure in between the dark cabinets and white marble, we tweaked the classic, urging it toward modern.

The chunkiness of that framework, the thickness of the countertops, the height of the cabinets—no dimension happened by chance. As in all of the best and most classic kitchens, scale outranks just about all other considerations in creating a successful aesthetic. Every dimension needs to relate and respond to every other, and perhaps this regard for scale is more immediately apparent in this kitchen than most. The gnarled timber beams have something to do with it. They define the ceiling in a profound way, providing a sense of protection while calling attention to weight and mass below.

This sense of solidity was an attribute we avoided in the cabinets. In lieu of wall cabinets, we opted for open space around the windows to let the windows breathe. An important detail is the lowered sill height—even or continuous with the countertop behind the sink—which allows for long views of the outdoors.

The open shelves flanking the sink window were an afterthought of the client's, but they contribute nicely to the feeling that this kitchen was collected over time. The openness allows sightlines and natural light to flow easily and makes the kitchen a living space that opens into a family room and then to the hillside.

This kitchen also opens itself to new thinking. The owners knew when to rein in their desire to design and create—they knew when to just say *non.*

14. **PARTY LINE**

When Jim Bakke, president and chief executive officer of Sub-Zero/Wolf, asked me to design a portion of the company's New York showroom, he said he wanted it to be done in an international loft style—and immediately qualified that by banishing exposed timbers and brick walls from his vision. This was to be the company's flagship showroom for its refrigeration and cooking products, and he wanted a refined and modern place to host clients from all over the world.

Jim and I have a lot of history, so it worked for us to kick-start the design process through a friendly game of storytelling. I played out this elaborate idea of the loft being owned by a man of the world, who, after a night at the opera, might bring back forty of his friends for desserts, champagne, cappuccino, a gorgeous view of Bloomberg Tower (which is the view outside these windows). I was not stretching the role of the showroom too far into fantasyland; the space also would be used for parties and events.

My idea included a more rustic than sleek interpretation of modern, something vaguely Asian. There would be a subtheme of fire and ice, which made for a nice visual pun with the company's duality of products. And the kitchen would be more than a workspace; it would be a living space, an idea whose time has come.

We ran with that fantasy and began by claiming the view. We centered the space with the Bloomberg building. The view feels like a giant piece of artwork. So does the roaring un-fire. Because there was no way to vent a real one and because a fireplace seemed right to anchor the sitting part of the kitchen, I designed an overtly false one (red-tipped flames of golden glass, planted in a bed of rocks), which was brought to life in a custom art glass sculpture by Chihuly Studio. Shelves for books and collectibles outline the fire. The facing benches (one curved, one straight) were designed to be deep enough for back-to-back seating.

As I do with a residential kitchen, I divided the space into compositions by function—cooking, refrigeration, cappuccino bar, and wine storage. We inset a pair of wall ovens into panels of wood and turned them into objets d'art. The range area got a floating stainless steel hood and a back wall of glass tile that resembles bamboo. An icy slit (of backlit and textured glass) pierces that wall and is functional, holding a couple of custom-designed utensil bars. The iciness continues in the nearby cappuccino bar where the back wall and sink area are art glass, again backlit.

The island was designed with a falling-edge detail. I wanted the brushed stone to look as though it folds into the dark cabinet and remains quiet, but provocative. I wanted the same demeanor from the adjacent, mosaic-topped sommelier table. The boldest element is the nearly eighteen-foot-long dining table, with a base that we made from antique Indonesian post holders and polished stainless steel pedestals, whose logistics proved equally compelling, considering this is the fifth floor of a design center in midtown Manhattan.

That table was not elevator-sized, and the crane idea was nixed. Cutting it was our only option. With a little wince, we cut the wood top jigsaw-style so the seam looks like a fine-lined crack, perhaps (as the story may go) acquired in a previous life in a palace in Indonesia. After all, we wanted a great space for a great party. We might as well go with the flow.

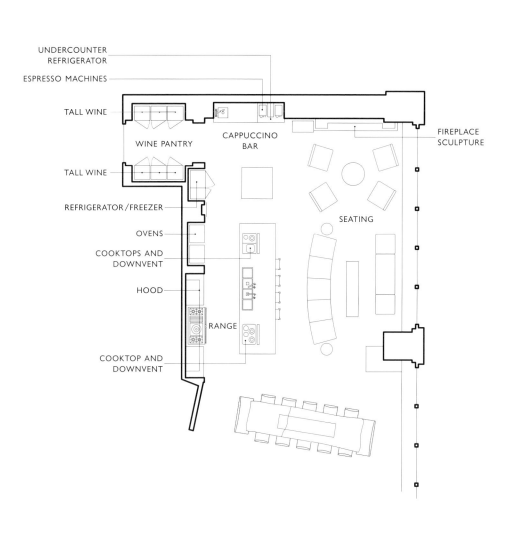

UNDERCOUNTER
REFRIGERATOR

ESPRESSO MACHINES

TALL WINE

WINE PANTRY

CAPPUCCINO
BAR

FIREPLACE
SCULPTURE

TALL WINE

SEATING

REFRIGERATOR/FREEZER

OVENS

COOKTOPS AND
DOWNVENT

HOOD

RANGE

COOKTOP AND
DOWNVENT

15. **CLASSIC**

I had designed test kitchens and corporate kitchens before, but nothing compared in size and emotional scope to this—the test kitchens for Meredith Corporation and notably for *Better Homes and Gardens*, its eighty-something-year-old flagship magazine and nothing short of a mirror into American home life.

This is where a cadre of culinary specialists develop and test recipes that are published in Meredith's array of magazines and books, and I was honored with the commission to redesign it in 2004. It would be the first redesign of Meredith's test kitchens in twenty-five years, and it was no small project. The facility, which exists in a three-story office building, encompasses about five thousand square feet and would include ten small, but fully equipped, kitchens; an herb conservatory; two dining rooms, one of which also functions as a library; and the crown jewel of it all—the showcase kitchen (complete with fireplace and sitting area), which is used not just for cooking but for hosting thousands of guests annually.

Karol DeWulf Nickell, then editor in chief of *Better Homes and Gardens*, was clear she wanted the kitchen to look and feel like a home kitchen, and she wanted it to be *American*.

With that mandate and the rundown of spatial requirements, I got to thinking about how to define today's classic American look—and how I could translate the essence of my client, which was not a family or a person but a corporation and a culture of American home life, into the design. I found answers by focusing instead on the notion of the American spirit and making visual associations with some key words: inventive, forward-thinking, warm, inviting, fresh, clean. I also liked the idea of a melting pot. The kitchen would mix materials, elements, modern, and traditional into a harmonious whole and not get caught up on matters of provenance.

We began by embracing our good fortune of great natural light. The space had ample windows and an attached conservatory—albeit aluminum clad and visually tired. We improved it rather quickly by cladding the aluminum on the inside with white-painted wood, which defined the interior of the conservatory and kept the eye from wandering outside to the parking structure. The conservatory suddenly became a glistening light box.

I carried the conservatory's outdoor feeling into the kitchen proper via the ceiling, for which I used a pergola-like rhythm to the beams and cross members. Like any residential kitchen I design, I then divided the space into zones—oven wall, range wall, refrigeration, *la mattina* (morning area), and island. And then I approached each one as a functional and artful composition.

I broke up the massive feeling of the island by flanking it with a baker's table at one end and a rolling cart on the other. The oven wall got a mix of closed storage and open shelves with an open niche in between. On the other side of the range and not exactly symmetrical with the oven wall, but pleasingly balanced, is the refrigerator/freezer in a cabinet of light anigre wood.

We opted for a light, fresh, earthy palette of materials that includes the anigre and also a brushed pine and a subtle taupe/warm gray granite. The range wall with its stainless steel hood and sliding glass backsplash, concealing storage for spices, offers a modern counterpoint.

The final touch: a square floor medallion at the entrance to the kitchen done in Italian *cottopesto*. I designed an organic vine pattern around the magazine's new streamlined (red plaid) logo. Our goal was to create a kitchen that felt fresh and energetic at every turn—and that is classic.

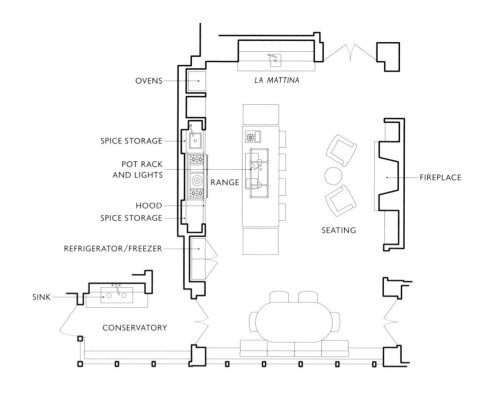

OVENS

LA MATTINA

SPICE STORAGE

POT RACK
AND LIGHTS

RANGE

FIREPLACE

HOOD

SPICE STORAGE

SEATING

REFRIGERATOR/FREEZER

SINK

CONSERVATORY

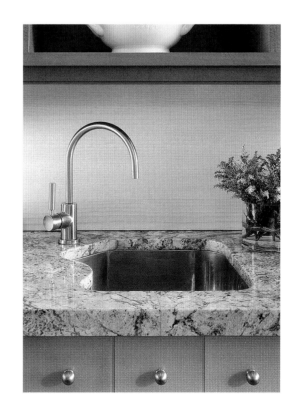

A classic is classic not because it conforms to certain structural rules, or fits certain definitions . . . . It is classic because of a certain eternal and irrepressible freshness.

— **EDITH WHARTON** (1862–1937)

16. **MELT**

MIAMI BEACH, FLORIDA

I often begin the design process by jotting down a couple of words to describe how I think a space should feel. Immediately, I wrote down "melt" for this kitchen in a Miami Beach high-rise that seems to have found that nebulous place where heaven and earth meet. One foot in the door, and I was swept into blue water and bluer skies. The panorama out those windows was incredible. I felt like I was suspended in a beautiful animation. And then another word leapt to mind: "decadent" (as in *pure pleasure*).

The clients—a couple of serious art collectors—handed me a good start toward pleasure in the form of a seventeen-foot-long painting by Alex Katz, an American artist associated with the pop art movement. Bucking convention that says fine art should not live near grease or water or fire or flipping pancakes or anything so corruptive, these clients were sure that their huge Katz would grace their kitchen.

I was intrigued—and onboard.

Where a window would normally be, this incredible piece of art would hang instead. And quite frankly, the kitchen needed a view of its own. (It exists as an interior space just off the front entry, where I designed a custom door handle in hand-hammered polished stainless steel as a herald of the artwork throughout this free-flowing, nearly partition-less condo.) The window wall to paradise was some eighteen feet away.

With the Katz established as our signature piece, the design fell into place. The entire kitchen would become a frame for that art. There would be nothing massive or overbearing in the space. Similarly, the materials, colors, and finishes would not compete with the painting. Everything in the kitchen would melt into the space. The Katz would preside.

The original concept (the one the clients nixed before I was called into the project) called for the kitchen to be drenched in dark wood. That was too heavy. The space needed to feel light, and when I think of a material with weightlessness, it is polished stainless steel. We used it liberally in the details and to face large elements such as the refrigerator and pantry. When inset into walls, those massive pieces now fronted in the polished stainless melt away. And the soft, dreamlike reflections of the Katz create a fantastic effect I could not have planned. The other key materials we chose—the light anigre wood for the cabinetry and Oyster Pearl granite countertops—also do not overassert themselves, but they exude a subtle warmth. This was a condominium meant for gathering with friends and family; warmth was required.

We purposely set the long table (a slab of reclaimed lychee with jagged edges, supported by two polished stainless steel pedestals) off center with the island to keep the focus on the artwork and not on any strong, axial composition of island-and-table. Kitchen essentials such as dinnerware and small appliances likewise keep quiet (and out of sight) behind sliding granite doors in a recess panel under the Katz. And we did not use any distracting light fixtures, either. Again, it was all about the painting. Light coves were developed throughout the condo and over the island in particular, to further recess the lighting and to wash the condo and the artwork prevalent throughout in a soft bath of indirect light.

Unlike many of my designs, this kitchen was not so much about mixing and creating counterpoints as it was about melding elements into warmth and light. That essence frames the painting and ultimately melts into the background. The Katz does the singing.

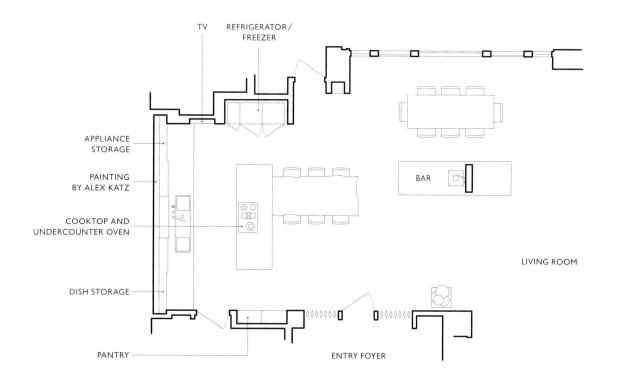

TV

REFRIGERATOR/
FREEZER

APPLIANCE
STORAGE

PAINTING
BY ALEX KATZ

COOKTOP AND
UNDERCOUNTER OVEN

DISH STORAGE

PANTRY

BAR

LIVING ROOM

ENTRY FOYER

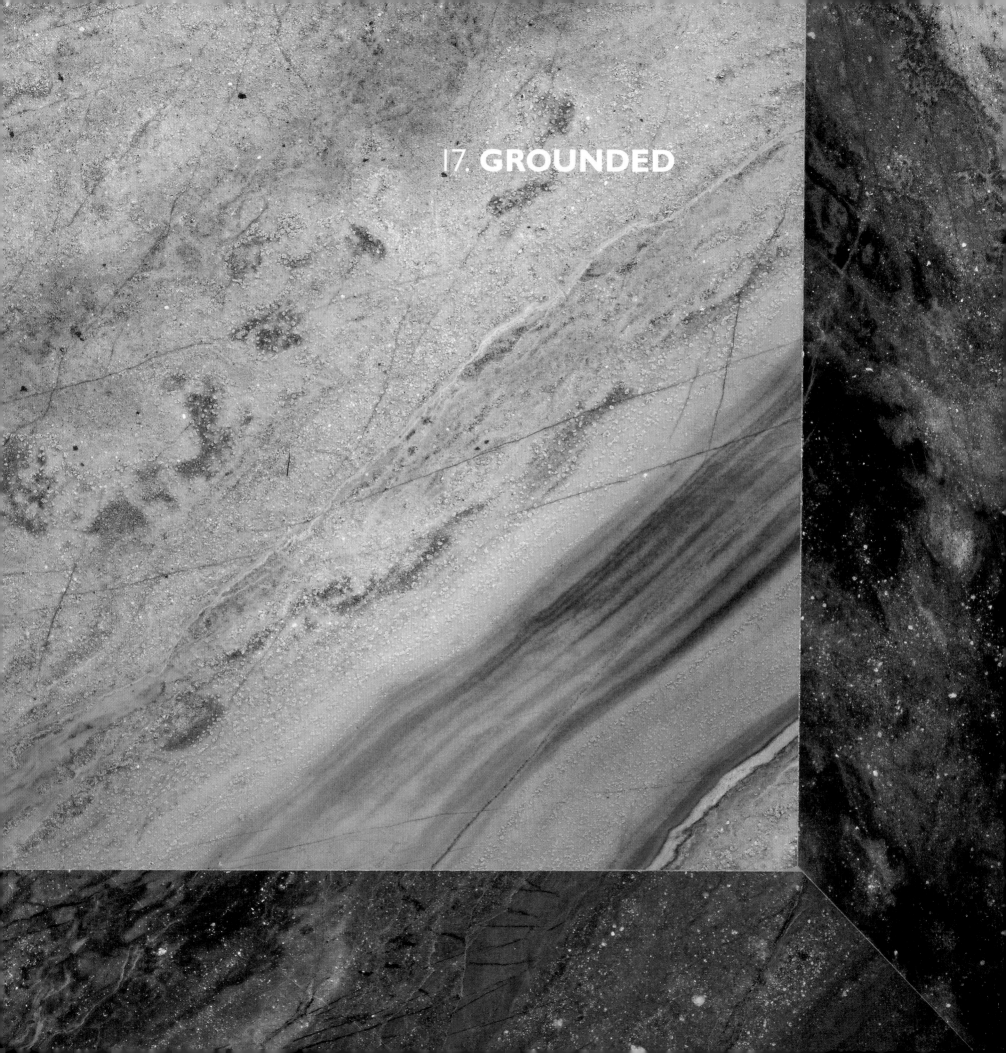

17. **GROUNDED**

SCOTTSDALE, ARIZONA

They had regaled me over the years with their stories of motorcycling and meeting artisans along the back roads of Italy. But such tales are not surprising from these clients, who always impart a sense of adventure.

She is an artist; he is not lacking in imagination either; and together, they *live* the talk. They like to create houses that push the norm and their own creative spirits.

So when they called me to do another of their homes, we knew we were going to have some fun. Their same builder and interior designer got the callback as well, which set up a fantastic creative exchange.

The clients—the woman of the house in particular, who was our artistic leader—wanted to bring the best ideas from their former home and then surge ahead. They wanted the breakfast nook they had before, the large center island, and the open space for gathering. They already embraced a kitchen centric way of living, but they wanted this new house (a 4,700-square-foot "old European" with a French flavor) to push the idea. They wanted the new kitchen to be more artful, more mixed, more potent.

The concept called for a kitchen/living space that sprawls more than five hundred square feet and soars eighteen feet to a gabled roof. A fireplace would connect above and below. A design theme should not exist. We even talked about the ribbing on the nickel silver range hood and how it should be fabricated without perfect pattern.

In spite of the awe of that kind of space and creative thinking, some real challenges presented themselves. We needed to make this larger-than-life room function efficiently. And we needed to warm it up without losing the transcendent quality.

For efficiency, we divided the footprint into zones made up of compositions within the greater whole. There is the morning area (*la mattina*), the island, cook area, and breakfast nook. To the far end, there is a walk-in pantry behind tufted leather doors. More cupboard space lives inside a black-painted armoire with feather pulls that we designed to look like jewelry.

Throughout, care was taken with scale and proportion (some countertops had to be thicker, the range hood had to be broad, etc.) to acknowledge the room's loftiness and ground it a bit.

We likewise paid attention to the humanity of the island, which was a monolith at more than four-by-ten feet. At the clients' request, we installed a magazine/newspaper bar at one end. And at the other end, a table serves as a welcoming gesture and breaks up the mass.

The granite top also needed de-massing. Instead of the usual seaming of large pieces of stone, we had the granite top fabricated from a series of sections with the grain directions playing off each other. To plan it, we took pictures of the stone slabs, cut those photos apart, and then manipulated the pattern of grains by hand as we moved the photo pieces around. In the end, we arrived at something far more interesting than a single slab would have accomplished.

Then we humanized that island some more, this time working from above. Inspiration came from my home where an antique Venetian ceiling panel leans against a wall in the living room. We had a similar panel built and painted by an artist and then suspended it over the island. It dropped the ceiling and brought the lighting down to a more functional level. It also sent a rush of warmth over the space. Or in more transcendent terms: it brought some of that wonderful mojo swirling about the ether, down to kitchen earth.

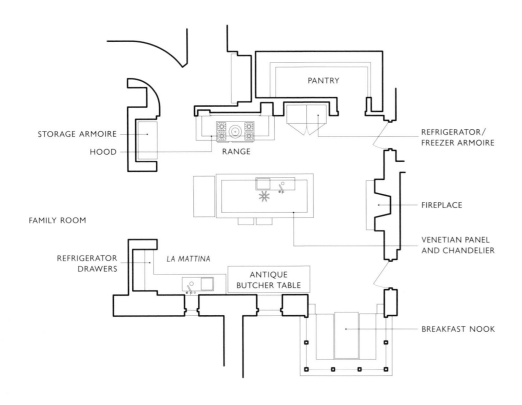

STORAGE ARMOIRE

HOOD

RANGE

PANTRY

REFRIGERATOR/
FREEZER ARMOIRE

FAMILY ROOM

FIREPLACE

VENETIAN PANEL
AND CHANDELIER

REFRIGERATOR
DRAWERS

LA MATTINA

ANTIQUE
BUTCHER TABLE

BREAKFAST NOOK

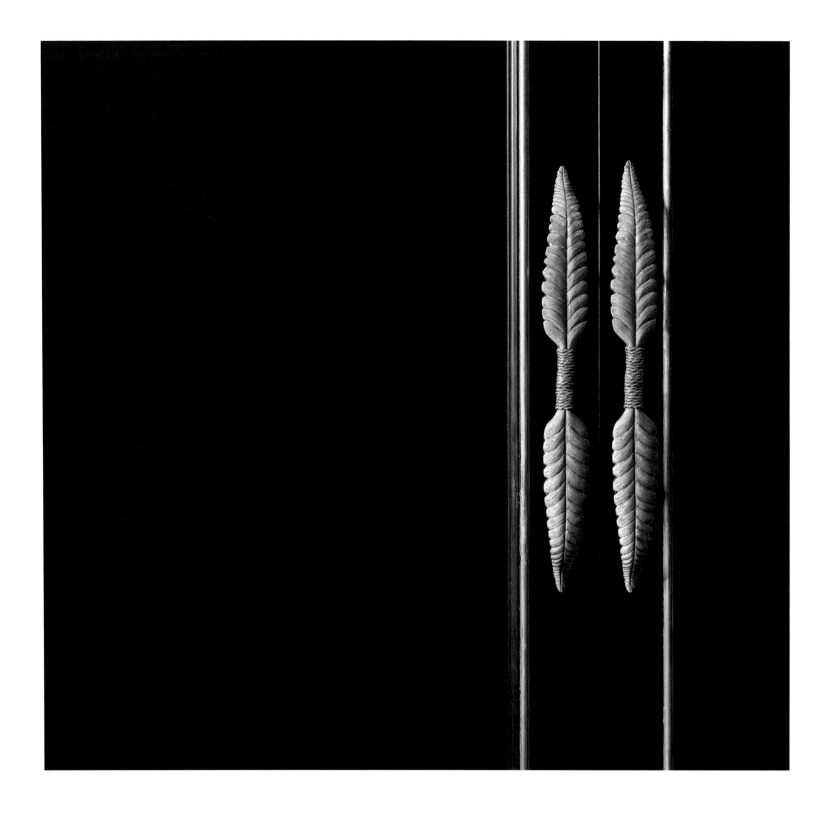

Do not go where the path may lead, go instead where there is no path and leave a trail.

— **RALPH WALDO EMERSON** (1803–1882)

18. **ATTRACTION**

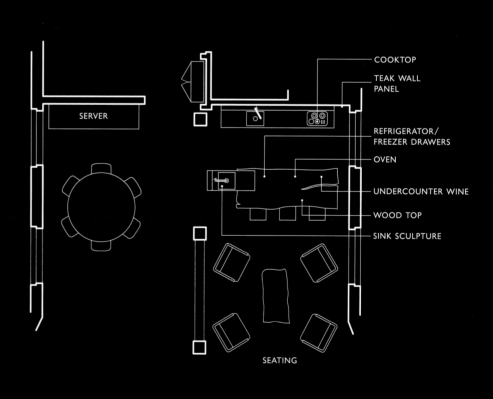

COOKTOP

TEAK WALL PANEL

SERVER

REFRIGERATOR/ FREEZER DRAWERS

OVEN

UNDERCOUNTER WINE

WOOD TOP

SINK SCULPTURE

SEATING

CHICAGO, ILLINOIS

Unlike most of my work, this kitchen resides not in a home, but in a commercial showroom, although the loft quality of the space could read as hip urban apartment. San Juan Ventures sells exotic and reclaimed woods from Indonesia. Think mango and lychee slabs, teak wall paneling, bendo root wall sculptures.

I knew the company and the owner well. I had specified their beautiful slabs and pieces for a number of kitchens, turned them into tables and flooring, and enjoyed the feeling that I had met the spirit embodied by those boards. And now the owner had asked us to infuse some of our spirit into a working kitchen on the showroom floor. This is where she would entertain her designer clientele and serve up exotica like lychee martinis.

The fact that the showroom space itself is a formidable species made the prospect exhilarating. The building dates to the 1860s and is classic, vintage Chicago (now planted in a gentrified neighborhood). The building survived the Chicago Fire and once housed a blacksmith and later a juice factory. That storied past lives on in the heavy timber beams, brick walls, stoic columns — and thus I knew the kitchen couldn't be anything but ultra-contemporary.

Inserting contrast or counterpoints (visual texture) into a space is one of my basic tenets of good design. In this project, though, point/counterpoint would drive the plan. There was a natural attraction (or should I say magnetism?) already in place that demanded to be unleashed. We would play old space with new kitchen, exotic Indonesian woods with slick materials.

But to start, we had to play it cool. This kitchen could not have its standard fare (range, hood, refrigerator) hanging out. That would overpower the showroom.

For an island, the client and I talked about cutting a stainless steel sink into a lychee slab — point, counterpoint. But both of us had second thoughts about permanently altering the wood.

So I came up with a stainless steel sink sculpture (inspired by the fantastic, almost futuristic forms of the Bolidism design movement that came out of Italy in the 1980s, in which shapes brought notions of speed and technology to life). The drain board cantilevers out from the body of the sculpture and slides atop the lychee countertop — although it appears to slice into the lychee. The highly polished stainless steel fools the eye. Under the lychee are two bands of dark-stained teak wood (one right under the countertop, one at floor level) that sandwich the island's stainless back panel. And again, the eye is fooled; the countertop appears to float. It is the same with the custom stools. The lychee seats seem to levitate; their thin stainless legs are barely there.

The major appliances perform their own disappearing acts. We tucked the wine cooler, refrigeration, and wall oven into the island's base. The electric cooktop goes incognito in a bank of white cabinetry along the dramatic back wall of the space, where we hung a large sculpture of reclaimed teak wood paneling, backlit with LEDs. Point, counterpoint again — the earthy teak and sleek white cabinetry (done in a manmade composite for further contrast) seduce each other. Another white cabinet, a secondary server with a razor-thin stainless steel top, likewise beckons its paramour, the earthy wood sculpture hanging above it.

Perhaps this project tapped into my woodworker's soul. Finding the spirit in each piece of wood is the ultimate goal, and this kitchen was all about unleashing soul.

DECODED

AIR 38

Cabinets: *Island and fireplace wall:* de Giulio Collection in linen white painted finish. *Sink wall:* SieMatic BeauxArts linen white lacquer, polished nickel hardware. *Range wall:* La Cornue base cabinets in black with stainless steel and nickel trim and spice drawers in walnut. *Refrigerator/freezer armoire:* de Giulio Collection clear pine in custom glaze, pewter hardware. *Open hutch:* SieMatic BeauxArts base cabinets in linen white lacquer combined with de Giulio Collection open hutch in linen white painted finish, white porcelain hardware. **Countertops:** *Island:* honed Calcutta Crystolla marble. *Sink wall and open hutch:* polished Calcutta Crystolla marble. *Range wall:* stainless steel. **Backsplash:** *Rotisserie wall and range wall:* American Olean white tile. **Sink:** de Giulio Collection in marble and stainless steel with sliding teak cutting board; Dornbracht faucet (Tara Classic) in platinum matt. *Pot filler:* Dornbracht (Madison) in platinum matt.

Range hood: de Giulio Collection in painted plaster. **Plate rack:** de Giulio Collection in iron with light oak shelves. **Pot rack/lights:** polished nickel. **Appliances:** Sub-Zero 700 Series refrigerator/ freezer; La Cornue range (Le Chateau) in black with stainless steel and nickel trim and Flamberge rotisserie in stainless steel with nickel trim; Miele dishwasher; Panasonic microwave. **Dining table:** de Giulio Collection in polished Calcutta Crystolla marble with bronze iron base. **Fireplace:** Lambert design in limestone. **Candelabra:** de Giulio Collection in frosted iron. **Floor:** limestone.

SEEING BLUE 50

Cabinets: *Island, window wall, server, and butler's pantry base cabinets:* SieMatic SL truffle brown. *Linen table:* de Giulio Collection in ebonized walnut, aluminum bar handles.

Butler's pantry upper cabinets: SieMatic in sanded glass, aluminum bar handles. *Apothecary:* de Giulio Collection in ebonized walnut, polished stainless steel hardware. *Range wall and wall flanking apothecary:* de Giulio Collection in stainless steel. **Countertops:** *Island, window wall, server, butler's pantry, and apothecary inserts:* brushed Cashmere White granite. *Linen table:* cottopesto in blue abstract with molten aluminum. *Range wall:* stainless steel. **Backsplash:** *Window wall, butler's pantry, and apothecary:* brushed Cashmere White granite. *Range wall:* Alulife bronzed aluminum panels. **Sinks:** *Kitchen:* de Giulio Collection in granite and stainless steel with sliding teak cutting board; Dornbracht faucet (Elio) in platinum matt. *Butler's pantry:* de Giulio Collection in stainless steel with teak cutting board. **Range hood:** de Giulio Collection in stainless steel. **Appliances:** Sub-Zero Built-in Series refrigerator; Sub-Zero 700 Series freezer; Sub-Zero 700 Series refrigerator drawers; Thermador indoor grill; Wolf double oven; Wolf rangetop; Miele dishwasher; GE microwave; Dacor warming drawer; Sub-Zero 400 Series wine storage unit; Sub-Zero undercounter ice maker. **Floor:** stained red oak plank.

General Contractor: T&T Construction, Willowbrook, IL.

COLLECTED 62

Cabinets: *Perimeter:* de Giulio Collection in butternut, knobs and cup pulls in antique brass. *Refrigerator/freezer armoire:* de Giulio Collection in maple with a custom glazed finish, iron pulls and knobs. *Butler's pantry/entry:* antique cabinets from Lucullus, New Orleans, LA. **Countertops:** *Sink wall:* Scoon Extreme (a French limestone). *Range wall:* Pyrolav in yellow mustard. **Backsplash:** *Sink wall:* Scoon Extreme. *Range wall:* Scoon Extreme with Gold Travertine herringbone. *Surrounding base cabinets/structure on range wall in main kitchen:* tumbled Giallo Reale travertine. **Sink:** de Giulio Collection in hand-carved Travertino Noce; Barber Wilsons & Company deck mount pillar faucet in satin nickel. *Pot filler:* Dornbracht (Madison) in platinum matt. **Range hood:** de Giulio Collection in painted plaster. **Appliances:** Sub-Zero 700 Series refrigerator/freezer;

La Cornue range (Le Chateau) in yellow with stainless steel and nickel trim; Asko dishwasher; GE microwave; Dacor warming drawer; Sub-Zero undercounter ice maker. **Antique butcher table:** Lucullus, New Orleans, LA. **Floor:** antique terra-cotta.

Architect: Al Jones Architect, AIA, Baton Rouge, LA; *General Contractor:* Gary Spurlock, Baton Rouge, LA; *Culinary Antiques:* Patrick Dunne, Lucullus, New Orleans, LA; *Interior Designer:* the late Nell Fetzer, Baton Rouge, LA.

HANDSOME 70

Cabinets: *Island, desk/TV, and la mattina base cabinets:* de Giulio Collection in high-gloss wenge, polished stainless steel hardware. *Range wall:* La Cornue in stainless steel with stainless steel and nickel trim. *La mattina upper cabinets and cabinets above oven and refrigerator:* de Giulio Collection in polished stainless steel with wenge interiors, polished stainless steel hardware. *Cabinets below oven:* de Giulio Collection in stainless steel, stainless steel hardware. *Pullout pantries:* de Giulio Collection, matched to wall finish, matte black iron hardware. **Countertops:** *Island and la mattina:* polished Calcutta Gold marble. *Range wall:* polished nickel. *Desk/TV:* glass topped wenge.

Backsplash: *Range wall, la mattina, and surrounding oven and refrigerator:* honed Calcutta Crystolla marble; walnut recessed spice inserts *(at range wall).* **Sinks:** *Island and la mattina:* de Giulio Collection in stainless steel with teak cutting board *(sliding at island);* Dornbracht faucet (Meta) in platinum matt. *Range wall:* de Giulio Collection in polished nickel with teak cutting board. *Pot filler:* Dornbracht (Tara Classic) in platinum matt. **Range hood:** de Giulio Collection in stainless steel. **Pot and utensil rail with hooks:** La Cornue in nickel finish. **Rolling ladder and rail system** *(la mattina and desk/TV):* de Giulio Collection in stainless steel combined with Bartels rail system also in stainless steel. **Pot rack:** de Giulio Collection in polished nickel. **Appliances:** Sub-Zero Professional Series refrigerator/freezer; Sub-Zero 700 Series refrigerator/freezer; La Cornue range (Grand Palais) in stainless steel with stainless steel and nickel trim; Panasonic microwave; Wolf warming drawer; Wolf built-in oven; Miele dishwasher. **Floor:** hand-scraped spalted maple.

BUTLER'S PANTRY 252–253
Cabinets: de Giulio Collection in high-gloss wenge, polished stainless steel hardware. **Countertop:** polished Calcutta Gold marble. **Backsplash:** high-gloss wenge. **Sink:** de Giulio Collection in stainless steel with teak cutting board; Dornbracht faucet (Meta) in platinum matt. **Rollout pantry cart:** de Giulio Collection in stainless steel, polished stainless steel hardware, and polished Calcutta Gold marble top.

Appliances: Sub-Zero 400 Series wine storage unit; Sub-Zero undercounter ice maker; Sub-Zero 700 Series refrigerator drawer; Pasquini espresso machine. **Floor:** black and white marble.

Architect/Interior Designer: Scott Himmel, Chicago, IL; *General Contractor:* BGD&C, Chicago, IL.

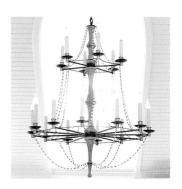

FEARLESS 80

Cabinets: *All cabinets (including island):* de Giulio Collection in alpine white painted finish, polished nickel hardware. **Countertops:** *Island and la mattina:* brushed Calcutta Gold marble. *Range wall and desk:* honed Petra Cardosa limestone. **Backsplash:** *All backsplashes:* Waterworks white tile. **Sinks:** *Island:* de Giulio Collection in marble and stainless steel with sliding teak cutting board; Waterworks faucet in polished nickel. *La mattina:* Waterworks in polished nickel; Waterworks faucet in polished nickel. **Range hood:** de Giulio Collection in painted finish. **Plate rack:** de Giulio Collection in polished nickel with white oak shelves. **Appliances:** Sub-Zero 700 Series refrigerator/freezer; Wolf range; Sharp microwave; Dacor warming drawer; Miele dishwasher; Sub-Zero undercounter refrigerator; Sub-Zero 400 Series undercounter wine storage unit. **Floor:** wide plank Eastern white pine.

Architect: Paul Konstant, Skokie, IL; *General Contractor:* Thomas Eick Construction, Ltd., Libertyville, IL; *Interior Designer:* Frank Ponterio, Chicago, IL.

NO PROBLEM 92

Cabinets: *Island, sink wall, and TV bookcase:* de Giulio Collection in Santos rosewood mahogany, stainless steel hardware. *Refrigerator wall:* de Giulio Collection in stainless steel, stainless steel hardware. *Pantry:* SieMatic SC10 with frosted glass fronts, stainless steel hardware. **Countertops:** *Island:* flamed Ivory Chiffon granite. *Sink wall:* stainless steel. **Backsplash:** *Sink wall:* Rimadesio Nuvola sanded glass. **Sink:** de Giulio Collection in stainless steel; Dornbracht faucet (Tara) in platinum matt. **Range hood:** de Giulio Collection in stainless steel. **Appliances:** Sub-Zero Built-in Series refrigerator; Sub-Zero Built-in Series freezer; Wolf cooktop with grille; Panasonic microwave; Dacor warming drawer; Wolf double oven; Miele dishwasher; Sub-Zero 400 Series wine storage unit. **Breakfast table:** de Giulio Collection in stainless steel with sanded glass top. **Floor:** custom wood plank.

Architect: Richard Gorman, Chicago, IL; *General Contractor:* Chris Carey & Co., Chicago, IL; *Interior Designer:* Barbara Gorman, Chicago, IL.

HORSEPOWER 104

Cabinets: *Island and storage stall:* de Giulio Collection in custom glazed finish, iron hardware. *Perimeter, including cleanup stall base cabinets:* de Giulio Collection in teak, antique brass hardware. *Cleanup stall upper cabinets:* de Giulio Collection in custom glazed finish, latches in satin nickel finish. *Refrigerator armoire:* de Giulio Collection in butternut, icebox hardware in mirror nickel finish. **Countertops:** *Island and cooking stall:* honed Scoon (a French limestone). *Range wall:* distressed nickel silver. *Perimeter:* honed soapstone; teak end grain butcher block top. *Storage stall:* maple. *Cleanup stall:* maple in combination with distressed nickel silver. **Backsplash:** *Range wall:* distressed nickel silver; Ann Sacks Elements ivory tile. *Perimeter:* honed soapstone. **Shelves:** teak with black iron wall brackets. **Sinks:** *Double sinks:* honed soapstone with sliding teak cutting boards; Harrington Brass bridge faucet (Victorian) in brushed nickel. *Cleanup stall:* distressed nickel silver; Harrington Brass faucet (Victorian) in polished nickel. **Range hood and pot rack:** de Giulio Collection in distressed nickel silver. **Appliances:** Sub-Zero 700 Series refrigerator/freezer;

La Cornue range (CornuFe) in stainless steel with satin chrome trim; GE microwave; Wolf wall oven; Miele dishwasher; Sub-Zero undercounter ice maker. **Dining table:** hand-scraped character butternut. **Floor:** wide plank calico maple.

Architect: Wright Heerema Architects, Chicago, IL; *General Contractor:* Preservation Trades, Inc., Wayne, IL; *Interior Designer:* Sheila Bradley, Evanston, IL.

RETREAT 118

Cabinets: *Island and surrounding column:* SieMatic 8008BR oak. *Range wall and la mattina base cabinets:* SieMatic 6006CG ribbed textured aluminum. *La mattina upper cabinets:* SieMatic sanded glass, aluminum handles. **Countertops:** *Island:* polished Giallo Saverkashi granite. *Range wall:* Scoon Extreme (a French limestone). *La mattina:* oak. **Backsplash:** *Range wall:* back-sanded glass panel. **Sink:** granite with sliding teak cutting board; Dornbracht faucet (Tara Classic) in platinum matt. *Pot filler:* Chicago Faucet in stainless steel. **Range hood:** de Giulio Collection in painted plaster. **Appliances:** Sub-Zero 700 Series refrigerator/freezer; La Cornue range (Le Chateau) in matte black with stainless steel and nickel trim; Miele dishwasher; GE microwave;

Sub-Zero 400 Series wine storage unit. **Floor:** hand-scraped character maple.

General Contractor: Chris Carey & Co., Chicago, IL; *Interior Designers:* Suzanne Lovell, Chicago, IL, and Christie Osmond, Chicago, IL.

SIDE SHOW 126

Cabinets: *Island:* de Giulio Collection in ebonized walnut, nickel hardware, polished stainless steel support base. *Dish storage base cabinets:* de Giulio Collection in high-gloss ebonized walnut, polished stainless steel hardware. *Range wall:* de Giulio Collection in stainless steel. *Dish storage upper cabinets:* de Giulio Collection in nickel silver with ebonized walnut interiors, crystal knobs. *Butler's pantry:* de Giulio Collection in stainless steel, stainless steel bar pulls and SieMatic BeauxArts amaranth, nickel pulls. **Countertops:** *Island:* polished Calcutta Gold marble. *Range wall:* stainless steel. *Dish storage wall:* honed Calcutta Gold marble. *Butler's pantry:* polished Oyster Pearl granite. **Backsplash:** *Range wall:* Veneto Niveus clear glass tiles. *Dish storage cabinets:* de Giulio Collection motorized lift-up panels in nickel silver with faux antique mirror. *Butler's pantry:* Modulus Shimmer tile.

Sinks: *Island:* de Giulio Collection in marble and stainless steel with sliding teak cutting board; Dornbracht faucet (Tara Classic) in platinum matt. *Butler's pantry:* de Giulio Collection in stainless steel; Dornbracht faucet (Tara Classic) in platinum matt. **Range hood:** de Giulio Collection in stainless steel. **Pot rack:** de Giulio Collection in polished nickel. **Plate rack in butler's pantry:** de Giulio Collection in polished nickel with walnut shelves. **Utensil rail on range wall:** La Cornue in satin nickel. **Appliances:** Sub-Zero Professional Series refrigerator/freezer and Sub-Zero 700 Series refrigerator/freezer; Wolf range; Wolf steamer; Miele dishwasher; Panasonic microwave. **Floor:** custom wood plank.

Architect: Andrew V. Giambertone & Associates, Cold Spring Harbor, NY; *General Contractor:* Kean Development Co., Inc., Cold Spring Harbor, NY; *Interior Designer:* Mariette Himes-Gomez, New York, NY.

BOOM 134

Cabinets: *Island, range wall, and oven wall:* SieMatic 3003E oak, stainless steel hardware. *Open shelves/artwork wall:* SieMatic SL505 oak, stainless steel hardware. **Countertops:** *Island:* honed Costa Smeralda granite. *Range wall and shelf:* stainless steel.

Backsplash: existing ceramic tiles.
Sink: de Giulio Collection in granite and stainless steel with sliding teak cutting board; Kallista (Vir Stil) faucet in stainless steel.
Appliances: Traulsen refrigerator/freezer; Wolf double oven; Wolf cooktops with Wolf downvent; Miele dishwasher; Panasonic microwave; Dacor warming drawer.
Floor: custom wood plank.

Architect: Vinci-Hamp Architects, Chicago, IL; *General Contractor:* NORCON, Inc., Chicago, IL; *Interior Designer:* Travis Clifton, Chicago, IL.

POP 144

Cabinets: *Island:* La Cornue in stainless steel with nickel trim; La Cornue olive wood baskets. *Perimeter:* SieMatic SL909 magnolia white gloss; La Cornue drawer cabinets in walnut flanking range. *La mattina, desk, and bar:* SieMatic upper cabinets in sanded glass and SieMatic SC51 base cabinets in magnolia white gloss. *Refrigerator armoire:* de Giulio Collection in custom painted finish, custom brushed nickel pulls, and polished aluminum knobs.

Countertops: *Island, perimeter, and la mattina:* polished Bianco Romano granite. *Desk:* walnut. *Bar:* cottopesto. **Backsplash:** *Perimeter and la mattina:* polished Bianco Romano granite. *Bar:* cottopesto. **Sinks:** *Island:* de Giulio Collection in granite and stainless steel with sliding teak cutting board; Dornbracht faucet (Tara) in platinum matt. *La mattina:* de Giulio Collection in stainless steel; Dornbracht faucet (Tara Classic) in platinum matt. *Pot filler:* Dornbracht (Tara) in platinum matt. **Range hood:** de Giulio Collection in stainless steel. **Appliances:** Sub-Zero 700 Series refrigerator/freezer; Sub-Zero 700 Series refrigerator drawers; La Cornue range (Le Chateau) in stainless steel with stainless steel and nickel trim; Miele dishwasher; Wolf microwave; Wolf warming drawer; Sub-Zero 400 Series wine storage unit; Scotsman ice maker. **Kitchen table:** de Giulio Collection antique bronze base with *cottopesto* top. **Stools:** de Giulio Collection in coffee bean finish. **Floor:** hand-scraped character maple.

Architect: Grunsfeld Shafer Architects LLC, Evanston, IL; *General Contractor:* Chris Carey & Co., Chicago, IL; *Interior Designer:* Suzanne Lovell, Chicago, IL.

MELLOW DRAMA 156

Cabinets: *Island, sink wall, and la mattina:* SieMatic BeauxArts amaranth matte lacquer, polished nickel pulls. *La mattina refrigerator/tray base cabinetry:* de Giulio Collection in nickel silver, polished nickel pulls. *Linen table:* de Giulio Collection in ebonized walnut, crystal knobs with polished nickel hardware. *Refrigerator/freezer apothecary armoire, small-appliance recess, and range wall spice cabinets:* de Giulio Collection in ebonized walnut, polished stainless steel hardware. *Range wall base cabinets:* de Giulio Collection in stainless steel. *Family room TV armoire:* de Giulio Collection in ebonized walnut with mirrored leaded glass, crystal knobs with polished nickel hardware. *Family room tall cabinets:* de Giulio Collection in ebonized walnut, crystal knobs with polished nickel hardware. **Countertops:** *Island and small-appliance recess:* honed Calcutta Gold marble. *Linen table:* SieMatic MosaicDesign Esplanade Amber. *Sink wall and la mattina:* honed Calcutta Gold marble. *Range wall:* stainless steel. **Backsplash:** *Range wall:* polished Calcutta Gold marble. *La mattina:* eglomise hand-painted glass wall tiles. **Sinks:** *Sink wall and la mattina:* de Giulio Collection in marble and stainless steel with sliding teak cutting boards; Dornbracht faucet

(Tara) in platinum polished. *Range area:* de Giulio Collection in stainless steel. *Pot filler:* Dornbracht (Madison) in platinum polished. **Range hood:** de Giulio Collection in stainless steel. **Plate racks:** de Giulio Collection in polished nickel with ebonized walnut shelves. **Pot rack:** de Giulio Collection in polished nickel. **Rolling cart:** de Giulio Collection in polished stainless steel with honed Calcutta Gold marble top and polished nickel hardware. **Appliances:** Sub-Zero 700 Series refrigerator and freezer; Wolf range; Panasonic microwave; Wolf warming drawer; Miele dishwasher. **Counter stools:** de Giulio Collection in ebonized finish with leather seats. **Floor:** custom wood plank.

BUTLER'S PANTRY 247
Cabinets: SieMatic BeauxArts base cabinets in amaranth matte lacquer; de Giulio Collection upper cabinets in nickel silver, polished nickel pulls. **Countertops:** nickel silver and ebonized walnut. **Backsplash:** faux antique mirror at sink, textured metal series mosaic silver tile at espresso station niche. **Sink:** de Giulio Collection in nickel silver; Dornbracht faucet (Tara) in platinum polished. **Appliances:** Miele dishwasher; Elektra Belle Époque espresso machine in polished chrome; Sub-Zero 400 Series undercounter wine storage unit.

Architect: Arnn Gordon Greineder, San Francisco, CA; *General Contractor:* Lencioni Construction Company, Inc., Redwood City, CA; *Interior Designer:* Joann James Interior Design, Menlo Park, CA.

RESTRAINT 168

Cabinets: *Island*: de Giulio Collection in ebonized walnut, antique brass hardware. *Refrigerator wall, sink wall, and pantry:* de Giulio Collection in ebonized walnut, rust iron hardware, willow baskets with ebonized walnut frames. *Range wall:* La Cornue in stainless steel with nickel trim.
Countertops: *Island:* honed Calcutta Crystolla marble and maple butcher block, corner angle hardware in antique iron finish. *Sink wall:* Negev Gold Light Jerusalem stone. *Range wall:* satin nickel. *Pantry:* honed Calcutta Crystolla marble. **Backsplash:** *Range wall:* sanded glass and stainless steel. *Pantry:* honed Calcutta Crystolla marble. **Sinks:** *Island:* de Giulio Collection in nickel; Waterworks faucet (Calais) in satin nickel. *Main sink:* de Giulio Collection in stone; Waterworks faucet (Easton) in satin nickel. *Pot filler:* Franke in satin nickel. **Range hood:** de Giulio Collection in stainless steel.
Appliances: Traulsen refrigerator; Sub-Zero 700 Series freezer; Gaggenau wall oven; La Cornue range (Le Chateau) in stainless steel with stainless steel and nickel trim;

Miele dishwasher; Sub-Zero 700 Series refrigerator drawers; Panasonic microwave; Thermador warming drawer. **Floor:** custom wood plank.

Architect: Michael Layne, Napa, CA; *Developer:* Robson Homes, San Jose, CA; *Interior Designer:* Renea Abbott/ Shappy Slips, Houston, TX.

PARTY LINE 176

Cabinets: *Island, oven wall, and cappuccino bar:* de Giulio Collection in sucupira with bronze hardware. *Linen table:* de Giulio Collection in sucupira with a polished stainless steel base and walnut lattice shelf, bronze knobs. *Range wall:* de Giulio Collection in stainless steel. *Wine pantry:* de Giulio Collection apothecary in ebonized walnut, light antique brass knobs. *Fireplace wall:* painted bronze finish.
Countertops: *Island:* brushed Colonial Cream granite. *Linen table:* SieMatic MosaicDesign Bellevue. *Range wall:* stainless steel. *Cappuccino bar:* Think Glass glass in Natura/Crystal. **Backsplash:** *Range wall:* Alulife glossy black aluminum panels, mixed-up grass patterned mosaics and Think Glass backlit glass art piece in Ice. *Oven wall and refrigerator/freezer wall:* Alulife glossy black aluminum panels. *Cappuccino bar:* Think Glass backlit glass in Natura/Crystal.

Sinks: *Island:* de Giulio Collection in granite and stainless steel with sliding teak cutting boards; Franke faucet (FF2080) in satin nickel. *Cappuccino bar:* Franke in stainless steel (PSX 110-16-8); Franke wall mount faucet (WMF 1280). **Range hood:** de Giulio Collection in stainless steel. **Appliances:** Sub-Zero Professional Series refrigerator/ freezer; Wolf wall ovens; Sub-Zero 400 Series wine storage units; Miele dishwasher; Franke Evolution 1 and Evolution 2 espresso machines; Sub-Zero undercounter ice maker; Sub-Zero undercounter beverage center. **Vertical column/side table:** de Giulio Collection in sucupira patchwork, Shagreen dyed cowhide and polished stainless steel. **Dining table:** suar slab and teak pedestals from San Juan Ventures, Chicago, IL, combined with de Giulio Collection polished stainless steel bases. **Dining chairs:** Christian Liaigre (Sellier) by Holly Hunt. **Counter stools:** Promemoria design, upholstered in fabric from Holly Hunt. **Small cylinder tables:** Promemoria (Edo) in bronze finish. **Fireplace glass sculpture:** Chihuly Studio, Seattle, WA. **Barcelona chairs:** Knoll in stainless steel, upholstered in fabric from Holly Hunt. **Round table:** teak trunk table from San Juan Ventures with Think Glass glass top in Minima/Crystal. **Straight and radius benches:** de Giulio Collection in bronze, upholstered in fabric from Holly Hunt. **Rectangular table:** de Giulio Collection in Tiger-Eye onyx on ebonized walnut base. **Floor:** sonokeling wood plank from San Juan Ventures.

Architect: Zingg Design, Middleton, WI; *General Contractor:* The OMARA Organization, New York, NY.

CLASSIC 186

Cabinets: *Island and range wall:* de Giulio Collection in brushed pine, stainless steel handles. *Refrigerator/freezer armoire and spice storage behind range:* de Giulio Collection in anigre, stainless steel handles. *Oven wall:* de Giulio Collection in anigre, brushed nickel handles. *La mattina:* de Giulio Collection in anigre, aluminum handles on upper cabinets and brushed nickel pulls on base cabinets; apothecary style front in sanded glass, stainless steel knobs. *Conservatory:* de Giulio Collection in stainless steel, stainless steel bar pulls. **Countertops:** *Island, range wall, and la mattina:* polished White Spring granite. *Oven wall:* polished Calcutta Crystolla marble. **Backsplash:** *Range wall:* sliding milk glass panels. *Oven wall:* interlocking bamboo glass tiles in yellow/vanilla. *La mattina:* brushed pine. *Conservatory:* soapstone. **Sinks:** *Island:* de Giulio Collection in granite and stainless steel with sliding teak cutting board; Dornbracht faucet (Meta.02) in platinum matt. *La mattina:* German Silver; Dornbracht single lever faucet (Tara Classic) in platinum matt. *Conservatory:* de Giulio Collection in soapstone; Dornbracht (Tara) wallmount faucet in platinum matt. *Range wall:* de Giulio Collection in stainless steel with teak cutting board. *Pot filler:* Dornbracht pot filler (Tara) in platinum matt. **Range hood:** de Giulio Collection in stainless steel. **Pot rack/lights:** polished nickel. **Rolling cart:** de Giulio Collection in oak with interlocking bamboo patterned glass tile countertop, stainless steel knobs. **Baker's table:** de Giulio Collection in iron with polished Calcutta Crystolla marble top. **Appliances:** Sub-Zero 700 Series refrigerator/freezer; Wolf range; Miele dishwasher; Wolf warming drawer; Gaggenau wall ovens; Sub-Zero 400 Series undercounter refrigerator. **Floor:** bamboo plank and *cottopesto* logo inset.

Interior designer: Joseph Boehm, Des Moines, IA.

MELT 198

Cabinets: *Island, sink wall, and bar:* de Giulio Collection in anigre, polished stainless steel recesses. *Refrigerator/freezer armoire and pantry:* de Giulio Collection in polished stainless steel, polished stainless steel hardware. **Countertops:** *Island and sink wall:* polished Oyster Pearl granite. *Bar:* polished Elegance Quartzite.

Backsplash: *Sink wall sliding panels:* polished Oyster Pearl granite with wood slide-out shelves. **Sinks:** *Sink wall:* de Giulio Collection in stainless steel with sliding teak cutting boards; Dornbracht faucet (Meta) in platinum polished. *Bar:* de Giulio Collection in polished stainless steel with teak cutting board; Dornbracht faucet (Inwall) in platinum polished. **Appliances:** Sub-Zero 700 Series refrigerator/freezer; Sub-Zero ice maker; Sub-Zero 400 Series wine refrigerator; Wolf frameless black glass cooktop; Wolf oven; Panasonic microwave; Wolf warming drawer. **Dining Table:** lychee slab from San Juan Ventures, Chicago, IL, combined with de Giulio Collection polished stainless steel base. **Foyer door/wood slats:** anigre with de Giulio Collection hand-sculpted door handle in polished stainless steel; ebonized walnut slats flanking door. **Floor:** marble.

Architect: CIC, Miami Beach, FL; *General Contractor:* Woolems, Inc., Miami Beach, FL; *Interior Designer:* McCann Associates, Chicago, IL.

GROUNDED 210

Cabinets: *Island and la mattina:* de Giulio Collection in butternut, antique brass knobs. *Refrigerator/freezer armoire:* de Giulio Collection in butternut, cast iron pulls.

Flanking range: La Cornue in antique white with stainless steel and nickel trim. *Storage armoire:* de Giulio Collection in custom painted/glazed finish, pewter pulls. *Pantry:* de Giulio Collection in pine, beaded board backs in custom glaze, antique pewter knobs. **Countertops:** *Island:* polished Verde Bamboo granite. *Flanking range:* nickel silver. *La mattina:* honed Calcutta Gold marble. **Backsplash:** *Range wall:* Giallo Reale travertine. *Sink wall and pantry:* honed Calcutta Gold marble. **Sinks:** *Island:* de Giulio Collection in granite and nickel silver with sliding teak cutting board; Franke faucet (MH280) in satin nickel. *La mattina:* de Giulio Collection in marble and nickel silver with sliding teak cutting board; Franke faucet (MH280) in satin nickel. **Range hood:** de Giulio Collection in hammered nickel silver. **Venetian ceiling panel:** de Giulio Collection. **Baker's table:** de Giulio Collection in hammered iron and honed Calcutta Crystolla marble. **Appliances:** Sub-Zero 700 Series refrigerator/freezer; Sub-Zero 700 series refrigerator drawers; La Cornue range (Le Chateau) in antique white with stainless steel and nickel trim; Miele dishwasher; Dacor warming drawer. **Floor:** antique reclaimed wide plank oak.

General Contractor: R-Net Custom Homes, Scottsdale, AZ; *Interior Designer:* Billie Springer, Scottsdale, AZ.

ATTRACTION 226

Cabinets: *Island:* de Giulio Collection in polished stainless steel and reclaimed teak, stainless steel bar pulls. *Sink wall and server:* de Giulio Collection in white high-gloss finish. **Countertops:** *Island:* lychee slab from San Juan Ventures, Chicago, IL. *Sink wall:* Zodiac in Cloud White. *Server:* de Giulio Collection in polished stainless steel. **Backsplash:** *Sink wall:* Zodiac in Cloud White; serpentine dark teak wall panels from San Juan Ventures. **Sinks:** *Island/sink sculpture:* de Giulio Collection in polished stainless steel; Dornbracht faucet (Tara Ultra Profi) in chrome. **Appliances:** Sub-Zero 700 Series refrigerator/freezer drawers; Wolf oven; Sub-Zero 400 Series wine storage unit; Wolf induction cooktop; Miele dishwasher. **Floor:** reclaimed teak from San Juan Ventures.

General Contractor: Arthur Westotowski, Lake Bluff, IL; *Interior Designer:* Real Simple Design, Old Mill Creek, IL.

PHOTOGRAPHY CREDITS

All photography by Dave Burk, Hedrich Blessing Photographers except the following:

King Au, Studio Au: page 197

Steve Hall, Hedrich Blessing Photographers: pages 13 (no. 10), 134–136, 138–141, 237 (right)

Janet Mesic-Mackie: pages 13 (no. 11), 33 (right), 149 (right), 150, 151 (top), 152 (left), 238 (left)

Scott McDonald, Hedrich Blessing Photographers: pages 13 (no. 16), 198–209, 240 (left)

Jon Miller, Hedrich Blessing Photographers: back cover, pages 7, 12 (nos. 1 and 3), 38–43, 47–49, 62–68, 70–72, 76, 77, 78–79 (center), 235 (left and right)

Paul Schlismann: pages 31, 246, 254, 255

Werner Straube: back flap, pages 4, 5, 27

Julian Wass: pages 12 (no. 5), 80–90, 236 (center)

James Yochum: page 35 (left)

All photostyling by Lauren Adel Klich except the following:

Carrie Costello: pages 13 (nos. 15 and 16), 186–195, 198–209, 239 (right), 240 (left)

Myrna Gustafson: pages 28, 29, 33 (left), 35 (right), 248, 249, 254, 255

Aurelia Joyce Pace: pages 31, 246

Gisela Rose: page 35 (left)

Hilary Rose: pages 4, 5, 7, 12 (no. 5), 13 (no. 11), 27, 33 (right), 70–72, 76, 77, 78–79 (center), 80–90, 149 (right), 150, 151 (top), 152 (left), 236 (center), 238 (left)

ACKNOWLEDGMENTS

For years, Karen Klages (now Grace) and I talked about doing a book together. I had always admired her talented work while she was a reporter with the *Chicago Tribune's* Home & Garden section. Her departure from the *Tribune* in 2009 marked the perfect opportunity for us to embark on this collaboration. She has been the true champion of this book, and for that I am forever grateful.

A very special thanks goes to my friends and essayists Chris Kennedy, Rachel Kohler, and Jim Bakke for their insight and contributions to the book and for their inspirational community and industry leadership.

I also want to acknowledge and praise my talented and dedicated team at de Giulio kitchen design. These are people who turn dreams into reality on a daily basis. Deserving of special mention are Greg Webb, who has been sharing his tireless and optimistic engineering talents with me for nearly twenty-five years, and Diana Fang, who retired in 2009 after more than twenty years.

And particular thanks go to Carrie Costello, the marketing director on our staff, for her discerning eye and attention to the details. She played a significant role in creating this book.

Heartfelt thanks likewise go to my friends and colleagues at SieMatic, especially to Uli Siekmann and the Siekmann family, and to Rolf Willers for their commitment to design excellence, their partnership, their friendship.

And a special thanks to *all* of the team who worked on *Kitchen Centric*, including the talented photographers at Hedrich Blessing—Dave Burk, Jon Miller, Steve Hall, and Scott McDonald.

I can't thank Hal Kugeler enough for his incredibly creative work on the graphic design of the book, and Lauren Adel Klich, our photostylist, for her elegant eye. I also thank Amy Teschner, our editor, for smoothing out all of our rough spots and for her wonderful candor throughout this journey and her colleague Kamilah Foreman, as well, for joining our team in the final stages to put her eye to the details.

It has been a pleasure to work with Balcony Press. I am most thankful to Ann Gray for shepherding us through the project, and to Peter Shamray of Navigator Cross-media, Inc., who brought the book to publication.

I am indebted to field editor Hilary Rose for bringing our work to the attention of national magazines. Special thanks go to all of the folks at Meredith Corporation for including me in many of their publications throughout the years and for providing some key photography. In particular, we thank Vivian Santangelo for her hard work in getting those images to us. A thank you also goes to the talented Julian Wass for contributing photography for one of my favorite projects in Glencoe, Illinois.

My deepest gratitude goes to my friend, confidant, and mentor, Dick Romano, for his continued faith and encouragement.

I thank my wife, Andrea, who I love very much and who has stood by me through each and every minute of my career, and my children—Lucas, Mickey, Briana, and Vinny—for their love and inspiration. Thanks also go to my parents, Mary and John De Giulio, and my in-laws, Yvette and the late Walter Fry, for their unending love and support and to my parents in particular for creating wonderful opportunities for me.

I wish to thank all of the interior designers, architects, artisans, and tradespeople who took part in these projects. And finally, I want to give sincerest thanks to each and every one of my clients—for their inspiration and for allowing me to be a part of their dreams. And I thank all of those clients who let us photograph their homes for this book, and for allowing us to share their dreams with others.

— Mick De Giulio

This butler's pantry in a stately home from 1929 in Chicago's north suburbs is in what once was a men's lounge that was graced with a beautiful window. De Giulio redesigned it as a butler's pantry and used simple white-painted cabinets and glass fronts. He designed the mosaic floor in a light green and white tile, in keeping with the classic style of the house.

AFTERWORD

Butler's Pantries

Mick De Giulio

They are often windowless spaces that feel like cells because they are small and tight and sometimes tall ceilinged with cabinets scaling those upper heights. They challenge a number of my tenets of good design, but I don't think I have ever met an old butler's pantry that I didn't like.

These are the precious anterooms of days gone by that link the kitchen with the dining room, and my favorite ones were designed by the architect David Adler in the early decades of the twentieth century. I have seen a number of Adler's beautiful pantries in the grand houses he designed around Chicago's North Shore, Adler's old stomping ground.

To my mind, these little rooms offer wonderful lessons in the marriage of form and function. They were spaces of the utmost utility. And yet, they also were elegant and odd places, all for good reasons.

Logic drove the use of lush materials in these rooms. Nickel silver sinks were softer than porcelain ones. Maple countertops were more forgiving than stone. In a room that held the fine china, those beautiful materials made sense. So did the lovely glass-fronted cabinets and abnormally deep (sometimes fourteen to sixteen inches) upper cabinets. The transparency allowed the woman of the house and her domestic staff to get an accurate glimpse of the entire collection of finery, and the extra depth in the upper cabinets was necessary for stowing chargers and oversize pieces.

There was logic, too, in their spatial eccentricities. The butler's pantry was a vestibule shoehorned into a floor plan, and that could mean it was located behind a staircase or in between jogs in the architecture. But these were real rooms—petite storage facilities and respites between the workaday kitchens and the heady dining rooms—where the finest china could live in harmony with the mechanical apple peeler.

Even though they are a room from a bygone era, I like to see a butler's pantry in a new home for those same reasons—high function, high elegance, high charm.

As a designer, I pour a lot of creative time and energy into these little rooms (and the occasional wine room, which is sometimes related to the butler's pantry in a floor plan). And, I have learned a lot from them, lessons that I apply more generally in my work.

I have learned that quirks are good (they give a space personality) and that when beautiful materials are invoked, one need not overdesign or overdecorate. Simplicity is best. Surprises are important, too; good design should induce a smile.

I have hung a crystal chandelier in some of the pantries I have (re)done, and for one pantry in particular, in a sprawling French Normandy house in California, I did much of the room in nickel silver, like a jewel box. And at my own house, I turned our rather amply sized pantry into what my wife and I playfully call the Pantry du Soleil (pantry of the sun). The room looks perpetually sunlit, but it's actually our glass-fronted cabinets gushing. We painted the interior of the cabinets periwinkle blue and then I lit them from the inside. We moved our family breakfast table into this space and sometimes use the pantry for intimate dinner parties.

The butler's pantry has inspired me in other ways, too. I designed a line of cabinetry for SieMatic called Hudson Valley, which is based on the simple, painted cabinets of vintage pantries. And the tall, freestanding cabinets that I design take their cue from the tall-ceilinged pantry, as well.

Small spaces are big opportunities. The butler's pantry is an example of that. But it is also testimony to the fact that when design is very good, form and function are one.

OPPOSITE
Inspired by high-function, small-spaced butler's pantries and charged with the mandate of doing something creative with Sub-Zero's wine storage units, De Giulio created this wine pantry in a wall for the company's headquarters and showroom in Madison, Wisconsin. The pantry (made of wenge with aluminum glass light dividers that are gently arced) raises the wine storage units off the floor by about fourteen inches (making them easier to access) and holds more than three hundred bottles.

THIS PAGE
For an eccentric French Normandy house in northern California (see also pages 156–167), De Giulio swathed the butler's pantry in white-painted cabinets and lots of nickel silver.

De Giulio gave a vintage house
in Chicago a new butler's pantry
in between the kitchen/sitting
area and the dining room during
a kitchen remodel. The ebonized
walnut cabinets are above motorized backsplash panels with
antique mirror insets.

In redefining the kitchen space in a vintage Tudor Revival house in St. Louis, Missouri, De Giulio created a bright, airy butler's pantry (shown opposite) that leads into its alter ego: an earthy wine pantry with ebonized walnut cabinets and a polished Wine River granite countertop (shown at right).

The incognito rolling cart (made of stainless steel and marble) is the surprise in this tiny butler's pantry in a French neoclassical-style house in downtown Chicago (see also pages 70–79). It was designed to slide under the counter. The clients use it to transport food and dinnerware to their roof terrace (via elevator) when they are not entertaining in the adjacent, formal dining room.

The tall cabinets (such as this chinoiserie) that De Giulio designs as freestanding pantries or as cabinets for refrigeration are inspired by the tall-ceilinged butler's pantry.

De Giulio likes to make his butler's pantries formal and elegant—with a twist. At his Chicago showroom, he created this classic pantry with maple countertops, a polished nickel sink and top, and lots of glass-fronted doors and then tweaked it with modern cabinets and a fancy crystal chandelier, both of which were not standard fare in butler's pantries of yore—nor was the motorized lift in the backsplash.

First Edition

Published in the United States of America in 2010
by Balcony Press.

Balcony Media, Inc.
512 E. Wilson Avenue, Suite 213
Glendale, California 91206
www.balconypress.com

Designed by Hal Kugeler
Edited by Amy Teschner
Printed and produced by Navigator Cross-media
Printed in South Korea

de Giulio kitchen design

1121 Central Avenue
Wilmette, Illinois 60091-2611
847-256-8833

222 Merchandise Mart Plaza
Suite 121
Chicago, Illinois 60654-1098
312-494-9200
www.degiulio.org

Library of Congress Control Number
2010924094

ISBN
978-1-890449-54-4